# COMMENTARY ON THE FIRST FOUR CHAPTERS OF THE GOSPEL ACCORDING TO MATTHEW

# COMMENTARY ON THE FIRST FOUR CHAPTERS OF THE GOSPEL ACCORDING TO MATTHEW

## AS PRESENTED PUBLICLY
## IN THE SCHOOL OF WITTENBERG

### BY

## DR. JOHANNES BUGENHAGEN OF POMERANIA

NOW PRINTED FOR THE FIRST TIME
BY ORDER OF THE AUTHOR
AT WITTENBERG
1543

as translated by
The Rev. Dr. Richard J. Dinda, Prof. Em.

Repristination Press
Malone, Texas

ISBN 1-891469-71-1

Published in 2016.

REPRISTINATION PRESS
P.O. BOX 173
BYNUM, TEXAS 76631

www.repristinationpress.com

# TABLE OF CONTENTS.

6

# Foreword.

It is a great joy to write this brief foreword to Dr. Richard Dinda's translation of Johannes Bugenhagen's *In IIII priora capita Euangelii Matthæum* (1543). This is now the second volume from the works of Bugenhagen which Repristination Press has had the privilege of publishing. Readers will find in these pages the same careful attention to detail witnessed previously in the pages of *The Public Confession of Johannes Bugenhagen*, but this time the Pomeranian's labors are turned toward a different goal: an explication of the first four chapters of the Gospel according to St. Matthew. Bugenhagen's insights have much to offer to the saints in this age, especially as he examines topics such as the responsibilities of Christians living under persecution, and also the parallels between the devil's attempt to tempt the Christ in the wilderness and the afflictions which have confronted the Church from the days of the Church fathers to the present age.

Next year, the Church of the Augsburg Confession will observe the five hundredth anniversary of the beginning of the Lutheran Reformation and as that occasion draws near, it is hard not to contrast the utterances of many 'Lutherans' in our age with the wisdom and fervency exhibited in the writings of Martin Luther, Philip Melanchthon, Johannes Bugenhagen, and their noble coadjutors in the Age of the Reformation. The dissipation of this theological heritage must be confronted by a willingness to return to the wisdom of that earlier age, and find again the courage to boldly confess the truth.

+*James D. Heiser, M.Div. S.T.M.*
*Bishop, the Evangelical Lutheran Diocese of North America*
*Publisher, Repristination Press*

8

# PREFACE ON MATTHEW.

When we must speak about the Gospel which reveals the righteousness of God, we must first speak about the Law and sin. Although the Scholastic professors may admit original sin about which Scripture speaks, nevertheless they weaken it in many ways, but some in one way and others in other ways. Moreover, Zwingli[1]—along with the Pelagians[2]—denies it not only wickedly but even very shamefully. In this way, those fall who boast of their teaching and yet, as Christ says, are not learned with respect to the kingdom of heaven.

In the beginning, therefore, we say that the person who does not see in Scripture the sin which we call (with just cause) "original," sees nothing. I am now omitting the writings which you all have in hand in our *Commonplaces* and in other books of ours and of the ancients. What is more clear than what Moses says about the beginning of the creation of all things: "God saw that all the things which He had made were very good."?

If all the rest of the things which God made were very good, surely all the more "very good" was man, for the sake of whom God had made everything else, for God made man after His own image and established him as the master of everything. He said: "You will have dominion over the fishes, etc." In his genealogy of Christ, Luke relates the origin of Adam to God as he undoubtedly makes God the Father of Adam when he says: "Adam was [the son] of God."

1    Ulrich Zwingli (1484–1531)—A Swiss reformer who is now best remembered for his opposition to the Lutherans on the doctrine of the Lord's Supper.

2    Named for the British monk Pelagius (354–420), the Pelagians denied the existence of original sin and taught that man had free will.

Therefore, just as Adam had to have been very handsome and sound of body, so also he had to have been very wise and holy in spirit and immortal without any sin. Can anyone who knows Holy Writ deny this? Now, however, unless you have lost your eyesight, you see that a human is not even "good," much less "very good," such as God saw him when He had created him. Later, God saw Adam not with different eyes but saw something else in the human being. Adam and Eve hence became fearful that God would see their shamefulness and wanted to hide from His face as He walked about in Paradise, but this they did in vain.

We read the following about the flood: "God saw that there was much evil of people on earth and that every thought of them was intent on evil all the time. He therefore became sorry that He had created man on earth, etc." Therefore, Adam, whom God had created as absolutely holy and who had a divine beginning, became the very wicked beginning for all his human descendants.

Here you see original sin, for no others can be born of sinful flesh than sinners who are blind by nature, ignorant of God, seeking their own goals, not subject to the Law of God, and, in a word, without the Spirit of God, and slaves to Satan.

Next, the punishment or judgment of God which we endure reveals original sin. The very wicked fruits of our flesh make clear the evil tree and our nature, corrupted as it has been by the venom of the ancient serpent. After all, man would suffer no punishment, experience no danger, bear no illness, nor endure death, had that original sin not been present on earth. Now to how many illnesses, perils, and other evils will we be subject? Harsh death carries off everything violently.

The fruits of original sin are blindness, unbelief, ignorance of God, neglect, contempt for, and hatred of, the Word of God, disobedience, hatreds, murder, evil suspicions, rivalries, very wicked depressions, corrupt emotions, etc. Our intellect has lost its sight, our reason has suffered perversion, our will has turned away from God. Without the Word of God, we pretend a worship of God. Our corrupt works lead us away from God and from the simplicity of faith which is directed toward Christ, just as happened to Eve. We live carelessly and believe that our faithlessness is wisdom and justice. We crucify the Son of God and judge that our persecution of the children of God is obedience to God.

Sin does not only madden us in our will, but even causes us to become utter fools so that we do not know reasonably what we are doing. How will the person who sees these things in people be able to deny original sin? Those braggarts don't even remember that they are humans! Here, however, I may define original sin as ignorance of and contempt for God, corrupt affections contrary to the Law of God in all people who have been born by carnal propagation from Adam.

In the meantime, the Law which God gave through the hand of Moses steals in here and there. Hypocrisy ratifies the Law as the remedy against death and dares to say: "I am not like the rest, etc." We, however, do not see the Law through a veil. Rather, it causes us to openly recognize our sin, faithlessness, impurity, and condemnation as it drives us to despair. You see, a good and holy Law is not good for me, for it is the sentence and judgment of God and therefore is death itself, etc. Thus, now that I recognize sin in my conscience, I know that I am sinning constantly and am suffering a terrible sense of hopelessness. That's how far I am from loving God as the Law has commanded, etc.

You have heard me call it an "ailment," but why do I say "ailment?" Up to this point, you have been hearing of our death. We seek medicine for a sick person, but we have lost hope in the case of a dead person. Let us now listen to the Gospel, that is, to medicine and life, which are impossible for humans but are possible for God.

The Gospel is the preaching of the remission of sins through Christ. We who believe this become righteous in the thinking of God and are the children and heirs of God. For "there is no other name given under heaven, etc." "No one comes to the Father except by Me. No one ascends, etc." Righteousness does not come from the Law but through Christ, if you believe. It is ridiculous that those who deny that original sin is a sin which condemns in the meantime want to teach (along with us) that we are justified by faith alone through Christ alone.

Meanwhile I hear the words, but they don't understand the subject matter, something which they would see even from one passage of Paul in Rom. 5. When we debate about the righteousness which is through Christ, we are also debating about our powers and works. Let us first consult the Word of God and believe that the Son of God has been given up for our justification. Next, let us apply that Word to counsel our experience, and let us ponder not how we have been affected thereby and not terrified by the judgment of God. Just as we believe that Word when we consult it in the true terrors and fears of our conscience, even when we are about to die; then, finally, we shall pass correct judgment about faith and works, and we shall teach others this correctly.

Here, however, I restrain myself from employing more words when we shall teach nothing else in all of Matthew than what he himself writes, namely, the salvation and eternal life which we have through Jesus Christ, our Lord.

I do not recommend Matthew, for he has been sufficiently recommended. He recommends himself not only with this book but also with this title as we shall say later.

# THEME.[3]

First, Matthew writes that Christ is the Son of God who was promised in the Law and the Prophets and that He came into our flesh for both Jews and Gentiles, namely, He who saves His people from their sins, and who was born of the Virgin and of the flesh of David according to the promise of God. Presently, in the third chapter, which is common to him and to the other evangelists, he begins with the preaching of John which reveals to us Christ, who with the Gospel and His wondrous works, reveals that He Himself is the Son of God in our flesh. Finally, Matthew brings forth this God and Man for us as our High Priest and only sacrifice for our salvation, who rose from the dead as our eternal King and eternal Priest and Mediator at the right hand of the Father. Our afflicted consciences will not deny that describing Christ in this way is the true Gospel.

# INTERPRETATION OF MATTHEW 1.

## "THE BOOK OF THE GENERATION, ETC."

With this title or inscription of his book, Matthew begins his Gospel, just as Isaiah and Jeremiah and most of the other prophets began their books and Solomon his proverbs, and John that revelation of his.

That title refers not just to the first part of this book, as some people think, but to the entire volume just as Matthew speaks clearly: "The book of the generation, etc." With this title, he com-

---

3    *Argumentum.*

mends to us especially his entire book and presents as his theme what we said before. Indeed, he wants to say this: "Let the whole world come. Let it see, read, and rejoice at the good things I am now writing, and let it know the happy news which is the Gospel. This book of mine is the book of the generation of Jesus Christ, who was promised in the Law and the Prophets and who for a long time has been awaited as Savior, and who will restore all things. In this book of mine, I write that He was begotten, became flesh, and came into the world. In our flesh, He declared with His words and works and with His very resurrection from the dead that He is the Son of God for the salvation of all who embrace Him through faith."

Here by the merit and command of God, He is called "Jesus," that is, "Savior"; for He will save His people—that is, those who believe—from their sins. This is the Christ or that Messiah or anointed One, whom Daniel calls "the Holy of holies" (ch. 9). In Him, all that legal and royal and priestly anointing (and therefore the whole Law) ceases. As John the Baptist says: "The Law was given through Moses, but grace and truth have come through Christ Jesus." In the Law, on the basis of the command and institution of God, priests and kings would receive anointing, and for this reason kings are often called "christs [or the anointed] of the Law." However, God the Father anointed this Christ, as we read in Psalms: "You have loved righteousness and hated iniquity. For this reason, God, Your God, has anointed You with the oil of gladness ahead of Your companions." Furthermore, the Holy Spirit anointed Him as the eternal King about whom God says: "Sit at My right hand until, etc." The Spirit also anointed Him as eternal Priest about whose priesthood God not only says and promises but even swears: "You are a Priest forever according to the order of Melchizedek."

As King, He has established us in His kingdom and defends the faithful against the Law, sin, the devil, and hell. As Priest, with His single sacrifice offered for sins, He intervenes for us at the right hand of the Father, as we read in Rom. 8 and 1 John 2. He also reconciles us sinners to the Father permanently that evil consciences not drive us to a despair over our salvation.

It is not the duty of the priest merely to *offer*, but also to *teach* the words and understanding of God. This Christ also does by teaching the Gospel externally by the ministry of preachers and internally by the comfort of the Paraclete which He Himself earned for us.

Who will not see that an absolutely certain hope has been presented to us in this eternal kingdom and priesthood of Christ? For, just as in this begotten and incarnate Son of God, we ourselves are the children of God; so also in this King and Priest, we are also kings and priests. As Peter says: "We are a chosen generation, a royal priesthood, an holy nation, a people who have come into gain, that we may preach the powers of Him who has called us out of darkness into his wondrous light" so that we who are now in Christ are conquerors of the world, sin, Satan, and death.

Therefore, you see with what magnificent promises in this title Matthew commends his book to us when he says: "The book of the generation of Jesus Christ." However, he makes the necessary addition: "…of the Son of David," which David is the son of Abraham. Scripture is in the habit of naming grandsons and descendants "sons," as you see clearly here. In this way, Matthew is looking to the promises of Abraham and David which they made about Christ (Rom. 1, etc.). He makes clear that Christ is obviously the Son of David immediately at the beginning of his book so that His genealogy follows in order.

Let us now gather from the words which Matthew has posited in this title the very certain arguments that this Jesus must be true God and true man, that He had to be born of the Virgin, that He had to die and rise again, that you may see still more clearly how this title pertains to the entire book of Matthew. Meanwhile, these arguments edify us while vain questions keep others busy.

After all, if the Son of Abraham and of David was begotten, He had to be true man. If He is Jesus, that is, the Savior, and the sort of Savior who saves His people from their sins, He is the true God Himself, because God alone forgives sins. Therefore, this Jesus is true man and true God.

Next, if these things are true, He must become a human not by the carnal process. Those come into being by the carnal process who are conceived and born in sin. How would He take away sin were He Himself be subject to sinning? Or how could He who is God and the highest righteousness be a sinner? Therefore God took upon Himself the begetting of Him by the Holy Spirit from the Virgin just as God made Adam outside nature without sin, and thus this man Christ was made by God outside nature without sin. The first earthly human being, however, was made of dirt; the second One from heaven, was made of heaven.

Also, if this true Man is from Adam, Abraham, and David, He must at some time die. If He dies, how does He overcome our sin and death who Himself seems to succumb? He thus must rise again to be Conqueror of sin and death; that is, truly Jesus.

In this same chapter, you have the same thing, namely, that this Jesus is the Christ, that is, the anointed One or the Messiah promised in the Law and the Prophets, that is, the One who blesses from Abraham, that is, the eternal Priest through whom all the nations of the earth would be blessed. From David, He is the eternal King who has all things under His power and even His enemies, the last of which is death, as His footstool. He would not be such, however, if He would succumb to the curse and remain in death. Therefore He had to die for our sake and thus to rise again. Thus I am not now saying that all that I have said had been foretold about the Messiah. If however this is the Christ, it is necessary that all these things be true in Him.

# ON THE GENEALOGY OF CHRIST.

In the genealogy of Christ, Matthew and Luke describe differently the descent from David, the former through Solomon and the latter through Nathan, the brother of Solomon; the principal factor and which alone we must respect is that Christ was born of David according to the flesh. It is this alone that the Evangelists want to express. Matthew was seeing that he had to prove or confirm this after he had said Jesus Christ was the Son of David, which David was the son of Abraham, that we may know with certainty that this is our Savior whom God had promised us through the Prophets; for he cannot be a true Christ who is not the Son of David.

After that promise of our salvation regarding the Seed of the woman (Gen. 3), which no one could see in some specific offspring of hers, and after that promise about the Seed of Abraham (Gen. 22), which would express a more certain offspring, as a result of which people would abandon the rest of the world and wait for Christ and which would neglect Ishmael and the other sons of Abraham who were not born of a free mother; I say, after these things it was said in the case of Isaac: "He will be called your Seed" (Gen. 21). After that, the promise signified even more clearly that the giving of Christ to us would happen through the tribe of Judah (Gen. 49). Finally, because in the meantime, the succession of the tribe of Judah seemed to lie quite open, God kept declaring that the very house and family of David would be the source from which the whole world must await its salvation (1 Kings 7, etc.).

The prophets often repeat this promise which God made to David, as Paul says, Rom. 1: "…who was made of the seed of David according to the flesh, as God had promised in Holy Scripture through the prophets." First, David himself sang many things about

Christ which we know well because he knew that Christ would come from his loins, as Peter says (Acts 2).

Next, Isaiah says, ch. 7: "Hear then, O house of David... Behold, a virgin will conceive, etc."; ch. 9: "...upon the throne of David, etc."; and ch. 55: "I shall make an eternal covenant with you, the steadfast mercies of David, etc."; as if to say: "You will have no need to say to God: 'Remember Abraham, Isaac, and Jacob to whom you promised to give a land flowing with milk and honey.' Rather, you will say: 'Remember David, O Lord, etc.'" The Lord swore the truth to David, and He will not have done that in vain: "I shall place Him who is the fruit of your belly upon your throne." That is, you will remind God and rejoice over the promise He made to David. So, too, in Jer. 23 and 38: "I shall raise up to David a righteous Branch, etc." God speaks in this way, Eze. 34: "I shall raise up over My flocks one Shepherd to feed them, My servant David. ... I the Lord shall be their God, and My servant David will be a prince in the midst of them." For He is not speaking about the person of David (for he had already left this life long ago) but about the Son of David, our Lord Jesus Christ, through whom God Himself is our Father.

Therefore, Christ is sometimes called not only "the Son of David" but also "David" in the prophets, as we read in Hosea 3: "Afterward the children of Israel will return, and they will seek the Lord their God and David, their king. They will fear the Lord and His goodness to the last days."

However, God remained consistent in that promise He had made to David. Never did He later express through His prophets regarding from which Son of David the Christ would come, although David had many sons from several wives. Because of the Messiah promised from David, the Jews very diligently wrote down the generations of all the sons of David very carefully and preserved them in the archives of the temple. Others also kept to themselves those generations which they knew especially were of the descendants of David, as Eusebius[4] writes in his *hist. eccles.*, Bk. 1, ch. 6, from the ancient writer Africanus, that people might be certain from what source to await the Messiah.

On the basis of these records, Matthew and Luke were able to write down the genealogy of Christ at that time. The latter, however, marks that descent through Nathan, and the former through Solomon, to Joseph, the husband of Mary. Luke lists the genealogy according to nature, but Matthew does this according to the Law. However, both do this from the flesh of David and weave together the genealogy from no other source.

What Lyranus[5] says is ridiculous. Moved as he was by a weak argument which he took from Pro. 3, he makes Nathan in Luke that prophet of David whom David adopted as his son, and that through him Christ came from David, something which is contrary to all Scripture. After all, adoption is a matter not of the flesh but of the will. Also, Scripture says: "...who was made of the seed of David according to the flesh" (Rom. 1, etc.). In 1 Chronicles, we read that Nathan was the son of David and the brother of Solomon. Why, then, do we abandon truths, invent fables, and fall into blasphemous errors?

You wonder which of the two is true: Whether Joseph comes from Solomon, according to Matthew, through the Law, or from Nathan, according to Luke, through nature; and yet from the flesh of David, whether through the latter or through the former. I respond. This is a strange situation to us. However, among the Jews these and similar points were well-known and common, and for the following reason. God had given them this law, as we read in Deu. 25: "When brothers live together and one of them dies without children, the widow of the dead man will not marry an outsider

---

4      Eusebius (ca. 260–340) was bishop of Caesarea Maritima. He was the author of the earliest Church history to have survived to the present.

5      Nicholas of Lyra (ca. 1270–1349) was a teacher within the Franciscan Order.

or stranger, but the dead man's brother shall go into her, take her as his wife and develop a connubial relationship with her. And the firstborn whom she bears shall succeed in the name of the dead brother so that his name is not erased from Israel, etc."

When Africanus[6] (whom we mentioned before and as we read in Eusebius) writes about the genealogies which Matthew and Luke relate in different ways, he speaks in this way: "Among the families of Israel, the names of generations are counted now according to nature and now according to the order of the law. Indeed, they considered the successions to be of nature which truly descended from the seed or blood, but of the law when some child begotten by another is substituted under the name of a brother who died childless. Because they had not yet received the hope of a resurrection, they imitated in this way a sort of likeness of a resurrection that the name of the dead person not be wiped out because of a failure or sterility.

"Because they therefore preserved the orders of generations in this way that some who were begotten by others because of substitution and some who were begotten by their fathers were reckoned by benefit of the law as sons; therefore, the individual Evangelists list the succession in both ways, so that one of them might explain a father as the one who begot the son and another as the one who seemed to have begotten the son. Thus it may happen that neither Gospel propagates a falsehood because the one follows the order of nature but the other follows the rule of the law. The families, the one which is brought down through Solomon and the other through Nathan, have been joined together so closely through substitutions which happened to those who were childless that nonetheless through second marriages one and the same child seemed to have been born from some parents but to be the child of

---

6      Sextus Julius Africanus (ca. 160–240) wrote *Chronographiai*, a history of the world in five volumes. It is no longer extant.

others. Thus it happens that both listings of the generations all the way to Joseph are drawn along very true lines but in a different way. This however is a sufficient explanation of the designated order."

With those words Africanus explains the law of Deuteronomy and speaks it absolutely correctly, unless someone should wish to bring the false charge that the Son appeared to be what the law says about the son. After all, He did not seem to be, but actually was the Son of the dead brother, although not by nature, but only by the Word of God who established the law. The Word of God, you see, is more powerful than nature.

After Africanus had said these things, he added the application thereof to the genealogies which Matthew and Luke recorded. In that application, he made some obvious mistakes, and these I leave to the reader to judge.

Before this law of Deuteronomy was written, the patriarchs preserved it, just as they had done in the case of other laws. (This we know from Genesis about the sons of Judah.) Later it was extended very broadly not only to genuine brothers but also to other blood kin and kin-by-marriage, as we see in the account of Ruth.

The legal succession in those two families of Nathan and Solomon could have happened not just once or twice through the course of so many years, for we also agree that the descent of Solomon ceased in Uzziah[7] and was restored by legal succession from Nathan. But when and how many times those things happened we now cannot tell with certainty except to the extent that we may on the basis of Philo. However, at the time when the Evangelists wrote, they could have indicated these things with certainty.

In addition to this law which Erasmus noted very carefully in Luke 3, it is enough for us to know what I advised from the beginning; namely, that Christ the Savior descended from David according to the promise of God and the utterances of the prophets.

---

7    Translator's note: Text reads "Ochozia."

When the discussion involved Jesus, our Savior, on earth, it is most certain and very well-known, even to our adversaries, that He was born of the lineage of David, for even the common crowd used to approve this with its outcry: "Hosanna to the Son of David!" The blind, too, cried out: "Have mercy on us, O Son of David!" In fact, even a Gentile woman said: "Son of David, have mercy on me, for an evil spirit is troubling my daughter." Also, although the scribes and Pharisees, who were the very learned adversaries of Christ, made all sorts of false charges and sought from every source testimonies from which to prove that He could not be the Christ, they would not dare assert that He was not the Son of David. It was, after all, very well-known that He was of David's line, and they feared that everyone would rebuke them as shameless liars.

Their false charges would include only these and similar ones: "This fellow is not of God, for he doesn't keep the Sabbath." Also, they charged falsely that it was a very serious matter in which nevertheless they were being deceived: "He did not come from Bethlehem, which Micah had foretold. He therefore cannot be the Christ." And: "He comes from Nazareth, but we have had no prophecy that Christ would come from there." This was because they didn't know or were unwilling to know that He had been born in Bethlehem, for which reason Herod had killed the children there thirty years earlier. How could they now have known this history, not to mention other things? He was only *raised* in Nazareth.

Some people say: "Doesn't Scripture say in John 7 that Christ came from the seed of David and from the town of Bethlehem where David was?" The question involves solely the town of Bethlehem and not whether Jesus was of the tribe of David, as if they be saying: "Let us grant that He is a descendant of David; nevertheless He came not from Bethlehem but from Nazareth." After all, John writes: "Some of them kept saying: 'He is truly a prophet'; and others: 'This is the Christ.' But some were saying: 'Does Christ come from Galilee? Doesn't Scripture say that Christ comes from the seed of David and from the town of Bethlehem where David was?'" A disagreement therefore developed about him among the common crowd."

The priests and Pharisees sank their teeth deep into this argument against Christ as very plausible, and a little later in their anger they threw it against Nicodemus. They said: "Aren't you a Galilean? Search the Scripture and see, for no prophet will rise out of Galilee." Those false accusers did not dare to raise this objection against Nicodemus, a very learned teacher in Israel.

Therefore you have it that Christ is the Son of David, something which Matthew and Luke wanted to reveal with their genealogies. Let us leave the useless questions to those who are unconcerned with this principal matter. Matthew goes down from Abraham to David and then from David to Christ through the fathers, because he had undertaken this task when he said: "[...the generation] of Jesus Christ, the Son of David, the son of Abraham," as he obviously looks back to the promises made to Abraham and David about the salvation of the world, which promises are in Christ. Amen. However, Luke looks back farther and goes backward or ascends from Christ through the fathers all the way to God Himself, whom he makes the Father of Adam, to show what we said earlier, namely, that Adam came from a very fine beginning, and that through his disobedience and through sin that became a very bad beginning for all the descendants of men. At the same time, he makes it clear that we return to God from whence sin had cast us into our damnation only through Christ.

But why do Matthew and Luke bring down the sequence of the genealogy from Abraham and David despite the fact that Joseph does not belong to the begetting of Christ and just as these Evangelists write clearly that Christ was born of a virgin? Eusebius responds in the passage we cited. In this way, the sequence is led down to Joseph by the genealogy of fathers. Thus we can entertain no doubts about Mary but that she was of the same family and tribe because according to the law of Moses, the tribes were not permitted to intermarry. Rather, an unmarried woman has the command to unite in marriage with a man from the same people and family lest through the mingling caused by [multiple] marriages the ownership of the inheritance be brought into doubt. It also was against the law to transfer the inheritance from one tribe to another.

Jerome also responds in this way and Ambrose does, too. Almost all the fathers that I have seen are of the same opinion. Jerome also adds this: "It is not customary for Scripture to weave the order of women into genealogies." Also: "This was once decreed in Bethlehem, namely, that the begetting be of one lineage." Ambrose, *Commentary on Luke*, speaks as follows: "The origin of Mary is also in the origin of Joseph, for, because Joseph was a righteous man, he surely took his wife from his own tribe and own hometown. A righteous man could not act against that which the Law prescribed." (Read Num. 36.)

However much someone might raise the false charge that we have said these things too simply, the Evangelists seem to be saying the same thing. The angel says later: "... of Joseph, the son of David"; and in Luke we read: "...whose name was Joseph, of the house of David." Why would they say and write this with such zeal if they were to judge that this had nothing to do with the lineage of Christ? After all, both had separated Joseph from the birth of Christ according to the flesh because they describe His mother as a virgin. Luke says (ch. 3) that people thought that Jesus was the son of Joseph.

Indeed, we could say that according to the Law, Joseph was the father of Jesus, because according to the Law, his wife was the mother of Jesus, just as according to the Law she was Joseph's true wife for she was a virgin who was betrothed, as you see in the Law

(Deu. 22) about the violated wife of another man. According to this situation, Luke could say in ch. 2 when His parents brought the lad Jesus into the temple: "His mother said to Jesus: 'Your father and I were grief-stricken and kept looking for You.'" However, Joseph could not have been the natural father of Jesus because Jesus' mother conceived by the Holy Spirit, and she, still a virgin, bore a child. Christ responds to His mother and to Joseph not about Joseph but to another and true Father and says: "Why is that you were looking for Me? You know that I must be involved with those things which have to do with My Father."

Furthermore, it is not enough for the two Evangelists to show the family of Joseph who was considered as the father, but they also indicate clearly the descent of Mary from David. Matthew quotes from Isaiah: "Behold a virgin will conceive, etc." But this sign, as we have it in Isaiah, is given to the house of David. Therefore, this virgin is of the house of David. Also, in Luke, Gabriel says to Mary about her Son, the Christ: "The Lord God will give Him the throne of His father David." How is Christ the Son of David if his mother is not of David's line and the Virgin who, without a husband, gave birth to Christ?

We have said these things quite carefully. Now let us look at the very words of Matthew and the sequence of genealogy which he describes.

(With reference to the genealogy of Christ in Matthew and Luke, read the second part of Luther's *Schem Hamphoras*.)

Matthew lists three groups of fourteen in this genealogy. The first order from Abraham is of the fathers or patriarchs; the second, from David, is of the kings; and the third, after the Babylonian Captivity, is of the now-obscure family of David and of the punishment of the extinct royal office among the Jews, for Christ had been promised to the fathers before the Law. Moreover, David had received the promise of a King and that He would come at the time when the royal family had become nearly extinct, as Isaiah foretells is, ch. 11: "A rod will come out of the root of Jesse, etc." Ambrose, *Commentary on Luke*, says these things beautifully: "In this way, the Evangelist has indicated the successions of changes. From Abraham to David, the Jewish people were without kings, for David began a righteous kingship. Next, through the kings he deals with every action of the Jews, and their kingdoms remained inviolate until their transmigration. After the transmigration, however, the Jewish nobility came close to the destruction of the degenerating people."

The third table of fourteen is not complete even if we count in Christ unless you should repeat Jechonias, for history has two men named Jechonias. One was the father, who is also called Joakim; the other, the son, is said to be. Jerome says this as follows: "Let us know that Jechonias is the first, and he is the one who is also Joakim. Let us know that the second is the son and not the father. The first of these is written with a 'k' and an 'm'; but the latter with a 'ch' and an 'n.' After a long period of time, these became confused among the Greeks and Latins. Otherwise you do not have this full slate of fourteen."

You ask: "Why did he set up tables of fourteen?" I respond very simply. Matthew would know that such lists were subject to quite easy corruption at the hands of those who are in the habit of making additions and of correcting the writings of earlier people. Therefore he sets up those three groups in lists of fourteen as if he were saying: "Whoever reads my book should keep himself along with me within that number that, if some smatterer should wish to make an addition as if to make some correction from history, he not corrupt the entire sequence of my genealogy and the truth of the account, which corrupters still often do who boast that they are editors."

For example, we all know from the accounts of Kings and Chronicles that here Matthew has omitted three kings between Joram and Ozias; to wit, Uzziah, Joash, and Amaziah. Nevertheless, no one has dared up to this time to insert these in Matthew. Not only ought we not dare do this in the case of Holy Scripture, but also Matthew clearly forbids this, for he testifies that he wrote only three groups of fourteen. And yet, almost everyone has judged that nothing of the truth is lacking from the account, were those three inserted. If those things which are written are true, as I indeed believe they are; and if the line of Solomon died off in Uzziah, king of Judah, I say that someone is injuring the truth should he insert those three here. I shall speak about this matter more clearly later.

Nevertheless, we are agreed that here in the first group of fourteen Matthew has omitted some between Joram and Ozias from the flesh of Solomon or from the flesh of Nathan or from some legal succession, and there is no doubt that he omitted more in the third table of fourteen. Nevertheless, it is not untrue that Matthew says that a grandfather or great-grandfather begot a grandson or someone of his descendants, just as it is not untrue that he says that Christ is the Son of Abraham and David, between whom there were many in a long list. After all, Scripture calls all older men "fathers" and all the descendants of the same tribe according to the flesh "sons" and "those whom their forefathers or the patriarchs begot." In the same way, it calls all blood-kin "brothers," just as you read in the Gospel that they were the brothers of Jesus according to the flesh and according to their clan.

You say: "If Matthew omitted some,"—as we agree—"what he says then, namely, that there were only forty-two generations from Abraham to Christ, is false." I respond. Matthew does not say that there were only forty-two generations as if he should have wished to list the succession of individuals, for there are more. With respect to his writing, however, he is being careful (as I have said) that none corrupt anything here with his own additions, as if he were saying: "In the genealogy which I now have listed, there are three groups of fourteen. I don't want anyone to remove anything from nor add anything to this under my name lest the multitude [of such "corrections"] produce confusion. Although we may be able to add more generations, nevertheless in my description there are only three groups of fourteen through which you can draw from Abraham with a straight line or direct listing successions and arrive at that point when God gave this sign in the house of David: 'Behold, a virgin will conceive, etc.'"

Again you ask here: "When Matthew says that Joram begot Ozias, why did he omit the three kings between them? For we are agreed that Jehoram begot Uzziah, and that Uzziah begot Jothan, as it appears from Holy Writ, and Jothan begot Amaziah, and Amaziah begot Azariah, who is also called Ozias."

I respond. As I said before, when Matthew wanted to place three groups or three states of time in the genealogy of Christ and only fourteen in each group, he had to omit some here. He was free to omit whom he wished, provided he advance by direct line and course successfully whence he was headed. However, Jerome thinks that there is a specific reason why he omits those and not others. For instance, Jehoram, because of his very wicked relationship with Jezebel, mixed up his lineage. Therefore Matthew wished to erase the memory of Jehoram to the third generation that he not place him in the order of the holy nativity.

Erasmus raises this not-inappropriate objection against this statement of Jerome. He says: "Let the diligent reader judge whether he should agree that here the Evangelist was offended by the wickedness of some kings because he pondered seating noble women ahead of them. Here I would be able to speak in favor of Jerome that he delayed for a long time sinners who came to their senses and turned to God away from those sinners who preferred to perish in their wickedness. Surely, which of those women would you be willing to compare with the very wicked Jezebel? Tamar only sought to have a descendant and did not fornicate afterwards. Rahab, the Gentile prostitute, converted to the God of Israel. Ruth turned from Gentilism to the people of Israel and was a very honorable woman. Although Bathsheba first was shamed because of her adultery with David, nevertheless she was a holy queen and the mother of Solomon."

Again, you might say against Jerome: "If Matthew did not list those three kings because of their wickedness, why didn't he omit other wicked kings later?" And thus, there will be no end of useless questions. The question here concerns the posterity of David according to the flesh. There is no question here which concerns the wickedness or saintliness of people. So what good is it to torment ourselves with inappropriate questions here? My response above to the omission of Matthew was the simplest answer and most pointed to the subject.

Note how terribly the posterity of the very wise Solomon (whom God had so gloriously exalted) perished because it had turned away from the Word of God to idolatry and the greatest foolishness, as David had foretold for it (1 Chr. 28) with these words: "Solomon, my son, know the God of your father, and serve Him with a perfect heart and willing spirit. For the Lord examines all hearts and understands all the thoughts of minds. If you seek Him, you will find Him; but if you abandon Him, He will cast you away forever."

Oh, that those who today defend the idolatry of the Papists against the truth which has now been revealed and become well-known might be able to see this example of the greatest king whom God had honored greatly and fear the judgment of God, because He killed the wicked King Jehoram of Judah and all his brothers with His sword as well a some of the princes of Judah (2 Chr. 21). Jehoram's son, Ahaziah, ruled for one year after him, and King Jehu of Israel killed him. In fact, Jehu also slew the princes of Judah and the sons of the brothers of Ahaziah who ministered to him (2 Chr. 22).

When Ahaziah's wicked mother saw that her son had been killed, she killed all the royal descendants (2 Kings 11), that is, all whom she feared would be successors in the kingdom. As we read in Chronicles, she slew all the royal house of Jehoram and occupied his kingdom for six years. In this way, the posterity and bloodline of Solomon perished. The Jews teach that Ahaziah had no son and that the lad Joash, whom Joashaba, one of the servants had saved and who succeeded on the throne, was not his natural son but succeeded from the blood of Nathan, the brother of Solomon, in the lineage and posterity of Solomon from some wife of someone of the aforementioned slain people, or perhaps from some queen who was the wife of Jehoram and had been left childless according to the Law of Deuteronomy which we cited earlier.

"But," you say, "Holy Scriptures say that this was the son of Ahaziah." That is true, and the succession to the throne was owed to him although Ahaziah himself did not father him. Scripture does not say that Ahaziah begot him. Perhaps it dared not say this when according to the Scriptural custom someone could be called a son for a different reason.

These things are very likely. Otherwise, why did Athaliah kill the royal seed if she had a grandson through whom she would have been able to rule and who would see the sons of her sons?

If these things are true, as I believe that they are true, and as the Jewish writers have always asserted and taught that the line of Solomon died in Ahaziah; you see why Luke was unwilling to put Solomon in the lineage of Christ but included Nathan from whose blood the royal line of Solomon was preserved by the law which Matthew describes. Also, if those things are true, you see how Matthew was unable to say: "Moreover, Ahaziah begot Joash." Perhaps he looked back to this when he here omitted several kings from the blood of Solomon. Thus there was no need for foolish and useless questions here by which you ask if he omitted anything. However, if you were to add this, you perhaps will corrupt Scripture rather than correct it, something concerning which I admonished earlier.

It is not in vain, then, that Matthew himself here forbade these additions to his fourteen-person lists. That you may hold the testimony of those lists to be true, from which testimony you know that those things which I have said did not happen long ago; I shall not be annoyed to cite here the words of the very renowned Jew Philo, for he speaks in this way about David and his lineage:

"When a quarrel developed among the sons of David whom he had fathered from Bersaba as to who should succeed David on the throne, David established by edict that this should begin from the youngest and that one should succeed the next younger when the natural lineage should fail. Therefore it began with the youngest, Solomon, and from the next youngest, Nathan, so-called son; then Ahiasar and Mathath and the descendants of Ahiasar and Mathath, Ahiasar or Achiasar. 'Ach' is 'brother' and 'Sar,' 'prince.' They were brothers of Ahiasar, the prince, who belonged to the succession of the kingdom. This was a gift for Mathath. That is, they received the gift that they all be called and be the brothers of the prince, after being gifted with a time to succeed. From then to Jehoshaphat and Ahaziah, the descendants of Nathan were always called 'the sons of Ahiasar.'

"Those whom Jehoram killed were the descendants of Nathan whom their father had honored in the tribe of Judah in addition to the decree. The sons of Jehoshaphat were said to be the brothers of Jehoram. The sons of Jehoshaphat were called the brothers of Jehoram. The infants of those whom Jehoram had left free in the tribe of Judah but were useless after their return were called the brothers and sons of Ahaziah, although Ahaziah nevertheless was the one and only survivor of Jehoram and Solomon. When he died, Athalia tried to destroy the whole royal line of descendants of Ahiazar. She would have accomplished this had not the youngest of the sons of Ahiazar been saved by the foresight of Joshabet, the sister of Ahaziah."

"This was the infant Elyh, who was also called 'Eliakin,' for Elyh, Eliakin, and Joakin are synonymous to Egyptians and Syrians. The infant Elyh was surnamed Joash, the first of the house of David and of the descendants of Nathan. From the time of that Joash and thereafter as a reminder, the kings always had two names. For that first who was called Elyh became Joash Simeon; also Her Manasseh; also Hezekiah Jesus; and names like that." So much for Philo.

It is pleasant for sinners to see this, namely, that Christ came from sinners, male and female; that He is the Savior not only of the Jews but of both Jews and Gentiles; that He is born not only of Jews but also of Gentiles because Ruth and Rahab were Gentile women. This is something that Luke very clearly wanted when he drew forth from Adam and his descendants the eternal Son of God, who became incarnate for us in time. You see, human nature is always looking for another Christ than the One who came from sinners, and who became sin and the curse for us, as we read in Paul. The sinner does not dare trust in Him as much as He has promised us. He does not believe that he is saved in tribulation when his sin upsets him. This is contrary to that verse of the psalm: "I was with Him in tribulation."

But now, on the basis of sacred history, we would have to say that in the genealogy of Christ we have something of the wrath and grace of God, about His promise, about His election and condemnation, about the nature of both the Law and the Gospel, about the Old and New Testament. That is, there is something here about our condemnation and the goodness of God by which alone He saves us for Christ's sake, as when Abraham had two sons, but Isaac was the son of the promise and not of the flesh as was Ishmael. For this reason, the children of the new covenant are born through the promise or election as was Isaac. Therefore, our desires are nothing to deliver us from the wrath of God. Instead, the promise given to Abraham is a great comfort for us, while, on the other hand, the temptation of Christ in the flesh and of Christians is very troublesome. We must rejoice greatly that the flesh of Isaac is sacrificed and that he is led by his own father to the death.

Also, although Esau was the first-born son of Isaac, when God called rather for Jacob, He said:"The greater will be the servant of the lesser." In this way again, natural birth is rejected, and God signifies that His people are not His people by nature but are the people of His election and mercy, not His children of the flesh nor of works but of His promise. He also signifies that the Christian people receive the gift of the blessing of the firstborn in Christ, the Firstborn, that is, the gift of the ministry and the kingdom, which blessing is the true Gospel of Christ by which they are blessed. Thus, all their kinsmen of the earth receive absolution from their curse, as God promised Abraham and as Luke explains it in Acts 3. Also, although the patriarch Judah had sons from his legitimate wife, these were condemned, and his family line was taken up from Tamar. Who will not be shocked at these judgments of God?

Again in the case of those whom God has taken up, who will not wonder at the undertakings and the goodness of God, which certainly is nothing else but goodness, for they indeed had no merit? When the twins were yet in the womb, by act of God they fought in her womb about the right of primogeniture, and the younger came forth before the elder. A crimson thread was tied on his hand, obviously representing the people of the Law, burdened by the Law, living in their own righteousnesses, because the Law is the ministry of blood and death. Fruitlessly the people of the Law try to deprive the faithful of their inheritance through persecution. Furthermore, Phares or Perez was not marked nor indicated, obviously signifying the freedom of the Christian people, and they would have a different justification than had the people of the Law.

We have already spoken earlier of Rahab and Ruth, the Gentile women, as you may see that in Hosea 1: "And it will be in the place where it was said: 'You are not My people.' There you will be called 'the children of the living God, etc.'" We Gentiles now are the people of God, friends of God, and the children of God, and this certainly not through the Law but through grace. On the other hand, in the sin of David and Bathsheba, who does not see the evangelical example set before the sinners when David is restored by grace alone?

We would have to say these and similar things, I say, and certainly with great fruit, from sacred history, but we shall hear them more happily from Dr. Luther in his treatment of the book of Genesis; and these matters will not be unclear for those who love the Word in their diligent reading of Paul.

Phares and Hezron were born before the children of Israel went into Egypt (Gen. 46); but Nahshon, the son of Amminadab, the prince of the tribe of Judah, returned from Egypt with all his people (Num. 1). To him and the rest of those who followed him, therefore, pertains the account of the departure from Egypt and the entry into Palestine up to the kings. Note here that God miraculously led the fathers into Egypt, miraculously led them out again and was never offended except by their faithlessness. Even when they did not believe, He cared for them. It is strange, however, that, after seeing so many miracles, after being protected so often by the death of their enemies, after being cherished by such great care of God, nevertheless they always left Him. But then, what else are *we* doing?

With reference to Salathiel or Sealthiel, see 1 Chr. 3; with reference to Zerubbabel, 1 Chr. 3 and in the prophet Haggai. After these, we have no testimonies in Holy Writ; but the ancients were very diligent in their keeping of the genealogy of David because of the coming Messiah who had been promised from the seed of David, as we said earlier.

Here we would have to count the seven periods of Daniel from the end of his discourse when Jerusalem would be rebuilt, as he himself says, all the way to Christ and its appointed destruction, for those seven ages belong to this third group of fourteen. But in his pamphlet, *That Christ was born a Jew*, Dr. Luther has explained those things sufficiently, as. Also, Dr. Philip [Melanchthon] has done the same in his *Chronika Carionis*.

At the end of this genealogy, we also must mention the prophecy of Jacob about the coming of Christ which reads as follows in Gen. 49:"The scepter shall not be taken from Judah nor the teacher from beneath his footstool until Shiloh come," or, as Prosper and the Chaldean interpret it, until the Messiah, or rather His Son, as others will say, come, to whom the people will cling. After Christ comes, the Jews will have neither kingdom nor priesthood. Where is their homeland now? Where are their sanctuaries? Therefore, let them know that the Messiah, who had been promised in the Law and the Prophets, had come from Judah and the offspring of David.

Regarding this prophecy, see the aforementioned treatise *That Christ was born a Jew*.

Matthew (1:16) calls Joseph in truth the husband or spouse of Mary although no man had"known" this virgin, I say he truly was her spouse because she had been betrothed to him. The Law, you see, considers a betrothed women a true wife even before they celebrate the nuptials, as you see in Deu. 22, where a man who violates the bride of another is guilty of death as a true adulterer. That is why the angel later says to Joseph:"Do not be afraid to take Mary as your wife." In this way, Mary is the true wife of Joseph, not by carnal union but by the Law of the Lord. As a result, one could say that Joseph was the father of Jesus not only putatively but also according to the Law, because He was born of Joseph's wife.

Furthermore, we could not call Joseph the father of Jesus according to nature, for Christ was born of a virgin, contrary to nature. This is what I advised earlier, namely, that it is not unusual that Scripture calls some "fathers" according to the Law who were not fathers according to the flesh and nature. In the meantime, when God acts in this way in the Law, we can later call this Joseph "father" without lying according to the Law of marriage, although this action, namely, the childbearing of the Virgin, may not have nor could not have an example.

God wanted His Son to be born of a virgin. Otherwise His begetting would not be pure, as we shall indicate below. He also wanted Him to have a legal father whom He could call "father" without lying, that Joseph might be His protector and guardian as well as the witness of His virgin birth and to make moot any suspicion of adultery that Christ might be able to say: "Who of you will charge Me with sin?" As I have said, we believe that to accomplish this, God formerly established that there be fathers of the Law or according to the Law who were not fathers according to the flesh. The Holy Spirit seemed to signify this in some way in the Law, namely, that there would be two peoples of God.

The one would be His people by nature, something which I say according to the word of Paul in Rom. 11: "If God did not spare the natural branches, etc."; and again: "All the more will those who are natural be grafted onto their own olive trees." The other would be His people by adoption "whereby we cry: 'Abba, Father'" (Rom. 8 and Gal. 4). In fact, as the situation stands, there is no natural Son of God, neither Jew nor Gentile, but only Christ. Believers, whether they be of the Jews or Gentiles, are the children of God by adoption and not by nature. Christ knew that He had a kindly-disposed Father who said: "This is My beloved Son, etc." Therefore we also consider God as such a Father, because He has adopted us in Christ and made us His children just as He made Christ His

Son. Understanding this is a very great thing and something we cannot understand unless we have regard for Christ. It also befits us to believe whatever we see in this.

It is truly marvelous that Christ is made equal to us and we to Him. John 1: "He gave us the power to become the children of God, etc." Therefore, we are now His children not by nature but by the grace of His Son. Therefore, it is right that our inheritance be the same as that of Christ. The Holy Spirit belongs to Christ; therefore He belongs to us, too. Just as the victory over sin and death befits Christ; therefore it belongs to us, too. Would that we understood this! Therefore, if we have been made equal with Christ through faith, let us also put on the form of Christ, who served us, that we may in this way serve our brothers. In this way, we all may become one with each other, just as God has made us one with Christ. This is love (Phi. 2).

# THE BIRTH OF CHRIST.

U p to this point, Matthew has been reviewing the genealogy [of Christ]. Now he is describing the manner as to how Christ was born of a virgin alone. He could and should not go on to say that Joseph begot Christ just as he had said: "Abraham begot Isaac. Isaac begot Jacob, etc." He first states the miracle and tells it in this way: "The birth of Christ happened in this way." Thus he separates this sacred conception and birth from all the others. You see, up to this time, He is and has been called "Christ," and He is the seed of Abraham, the seed of Jacob, the seed of David, etc., and thus is also the seed or son of Adam, as Luke calls Him. He is true man, which He Himself indicates in the manner of Scripture as often as He calls Himself "the Son of Man" in the Evangelists. When Matthew reaches this very birth of Christ, he therefore excludes the seed of man and therefore a husband or father according to the flesh. The eternal Father produces by effect of the Holy Spirit from the Virgin Mary, the daughter of Abraham and David, that blessed Seed of Abraham for us. He is the blessing of all nations, that is, His eternal Son, now become a man in time from the Virgin that through Him all nations who were lying subject to the curse from Adam might receive the forgiveness of their sins and an eternal blessing, just as the Father had promised Abraham when He said: "In your seed all nations of the earth will be called blessed."

Why is it that God promises all people a blessing unless all people have been cursed before God through the disobedience of one man, Adam? But how could they be blessed, that is, delivered from their curse, through this one Seed of Abraham if this Seed were conceived and born just as others who say: "Behold, O Lord, I was shaped from an unclean seed, and my mother conceived me in sin."? Indeed, the Son of God became flesh, that is, He became a true man, on our behalf, but not in a carnal manner from the concupiscence of the flesh, that I not say that this did not befit the Son of God.

It thus was necessary that this flesh be conceived from the Holy Spirit, and for this work God ordained the Virgin to be His mother that that conception and birth have nothing unclean. This was going to be the blessing for all of us cursed people, and there is salvation in no one else. In this way, you may see how the promise of Abraham which was also made to the fathers looks to the Virgin mother of this blessed Seed, and in like fashion also to the death, resurrection, and eternal kingdom of Christ.

If Christ is the true Seed of Abraham, He must die. And if He Himself is a blessing for others (as we read in Psa. 20), it is impossible for death to hold Him who is the curse, as Peter says (Acts 2). Neither sin nor death will be able to have dominion over Him to hold Him captive, although He underwent these temporarily for us. Although such promises about Christ may look to His virgin mother, God also wanted to relate this expressly and finally to the house of David, for He says in Isa. 7: "Hear, O house of David, the Lord Himself will give you a sign. Behold, a virgin will conceive, etc."

This prophecy and wondrous sign agree with the first promise of God made to the first parents: "The very seed of the woman will bruise the head of the serpent," that is, the kingdom of the devil, sin, death, and hell, to which we all have been damned. What else is the Seed of the woman, which is not the seed of her husband? We told earlier the remaining things which follow from the words of such prophecies and promises about Christ as that this Son is true God and true man, pure, mortal, and is going to rise again.

In this Gospel, Matthew first describes for us the Person of Christ, that is, who and what Christ is, namely, true God and true man, without any sin. As true God, He is called not only Emmanuel, but He is also said to be going to save His people from their sins, something which is the work of God alone. He is also true man. As He fills the lap of the little lady, He is her true Son, for the prophet says: "A virgin will bear a son," surely not someone else's son but her own, just as the Evangelist says clearly: "She bore her firstborn Son," but this she did without sin, for you read that He was conceived by the Holy Spirit and was born of the Virgin. Paul says that this Man was from Adam. He therefore separated Him from all other people when he says: "The second Man is heavenly and from heaven."

We therefore confess that there are two natures, divine and human, inseparably in the one Person of Christ, and now the Son of God and the son of Mary are one Son, one Person. Therefore Scripture and our confession of faith do not divide this Person in their words. What befits the one nature they assert about the entire Person of Christ. Thus, the Son of the Virgin is God and the Son of God because "the Word was made flesh," etc. Thus we confess that the Son of God, our one Lord, "was conceived by the Holy Spirit, born of the Virgin Mary, suffered under Pontius Pilate, was crucified, died, and was buried, descended into hell, rose again from the dead, ascended into heaven and sits at the right hand of God where He will judge..." He Himself says, John 3: "No one ascends into heaven except the One who descended from heaven, the Son of man who is in heaven." And in John 6: "What if you see the Son of man ascending into heaven where He was before?" All Scripture speaks about Christ, at the same time God and man, in this way. Gen. 3: "The Seed of the woman (which surely is a man) will bruise the head of the serpent (something which is the work of God)." Gen. 22: "In the seed of Abraham (You see the man.) all nations of the earth will be blessed (This is the work of God.)." Paul explains this in 2 Cor. 5, where he says: "God was in Christ, reconciling the world unto Himself, not imputing to it its sins." Peter explains it to the Jews in Acts 3, where he says: "God sent first to you His Son Jesus, whom He had raised to bless you so that each of you might turn away from his iniquities." In Jer. 33, we read that the Branch of David will be called "God, our Justifier"; and in Isa. 9, that the little Child will be called "El," that is, the God and Father of the coming age, etc. In Isa. 11, we read that the nations will place their hope in the One who rises from the root of Jesse. In Acts 20, Paul therefore dares to say to the bishops of the Ephesians: "Pay attention to yourselves and to the entire flock over which the Holy Spirit has placed you as bishops to rule the Church of God which He acquired with His blood." That blood is the blood of Him who is God, namely, Christ. He therefore is correct in calling it "the blood of God."

The catholic teachers have taught and defended these things from Holy Scripture against heretics who believe otherwise. The blessed Cyril writes to Successus: "We assert fully that a union of the two natures had occurred, and yet we confess absolutely correctly that there is one Son, one God, for 'the Word became flesh.' After the union the flesh was carried off into two by a division. We believe now that there is one substance of the Son but now that that is the substance of the One who was made man and incarnate. You see, when we inquire curiously into the manner of the incarnation, the human mind has agreed that the two are united indescribably without mixing, according to a united condition. The human mind undoubtedly looks carefully at this but believes and accepts steadfastly that Christ the Lord is the one Son of God from both [God and man]. Therefore, we recognize His one Person, but we acknowledge the difference of words when we say things according to the deity of Christ and other things about the humanity of Christ. We, however, make no division after the union of the two natures." So much for Cyril.

We must know these things and believe and confess them firmly not only against heretics and wicked teachers—some of whom have denied the divinity of Christ and others the true humanity of Christ—but also for the strengthening of our own faith. You see, the Christ whom God the Father has given us is the sort who wants and is able to help us because He wants and is able to be a man like us because He is true God. Such a God would be appropriate to be our Chief Priest, etc., as we read in the epistle to the Hebrews.

Second, in this Gospel, Matthew presents to us through these very words which we have spoken the true use of this Person or of Christ, who is God and man, and why God gave Him to us or why He came to us. This is the actual good news, namely, that He is Immanuel (that is, God with us), not only like us now in our flesh but also that He does not condemn us through the Law, which condemns sinners and makes them guilty of eternal judgment. He neither is against us nor is He far from us, as we read in Psalms. Salvation is far from the wicked but He is with us, as John says. He has lived among us, and as God and man, He is on our side and is our Mediator between man and God. At the same time, He is also Jesus, that is, the Savior or Preserver, who not only saves and defends His people with political peace but also, as the angel says, "saves His people from their sins."

Because of our sins, the Law has condemned us to eternal death. There is no remedy for us in the works and powers of ourselves nor of any other creature either in heaven or on earth. Because of false confidence we can become worse and even more blind so that it is impossible for us to receive help. Christ alone saves, and He does not save all but only His own people (that is, those who believe in Him) from their sins. As John the Baptist says, John 3: "He who believes in the Son has eternal life, but he who does not believe in the Son, the wrath of God remains upon him." Peter says, Acts 3: "There is no other name under heaven given among men in which we must be saved."

When, then, you have become acquainted with the Person of Christ, namely, that He is true God and true man, come and learn also the use of such knowledge, for the devil also knows the former, but not the latter, for he knows that the Christ was not given to him for salvation. Moreover, we must understand that the Child was born for us, and the Son was given to us, as Isaiah foretold. I am not giving you advice in vain, for what advantage becomes yours to debate about a great treasure which you have no permission to use?

Heretics have compelled truthful teachers to defend necessarily the Person of Christ with their faith and on the basis of Holy Scripture; that is, His true divinity and absolutely pure humanity as well as the article on the indescribable Trinity. Thus, they rarely are free to deal with the use of Christ or the article of justification. Nevertheless, if you do not know that article, what is the benefit for you to speak eloquently about the person of Christ—something which the devil also knows? James himself says that the evil spirits believe and tremble at Him. To know the use of Christ whom the Father has given us is to know the true Gospel and therefore to have eternal life.

# ON SOME WORDS OF MATTHEW HERE.

In Matthew 19, Christ speaks about marriage, which God created and instituted. However, we wonder at the insane blasphemy of the Papists who defend the doctrines of demons (as Paul calls them), namely, for adorning and commending their impure celibacy in which they are neither virgins nor chaste. They produce as examples John the Baptist, filled as he was with the Holy Spirit from the womb of his mother and whom God sent, according to the prophecy of the prophet, not to be the husband of the household but to be the voice crying in the wilderness; and the Virgin Mary, overshadowed by the Holy Spirit for this, namely, to be the mother of God. These are pure and outstanding miracles of God and personal privileges which we must not oppose to the general arrangement of God, and to which we must not oppose even the fact that some people, however great sinners they otherwise may have been, received by singular privilege and gift of God the gift of continence, that is, of living chastely in body and mind, as Paul says.

These people may use their gift if they wish and even rejoice in it. However, they should not disturb others, nor confirm the doctrines of demons to us. They indeed even dare to bring up the example of Christ in support of themselves because He was not a husband and remained a virgin. By God, how shameful it is to bring up the very great mystery of the divine dignity and of this most holy incarnation of the Son of God as doctrines of demons who forbid marriage!

In the meantime, they are unwilling to see here how the Son of God wanted us to honor very greatly not some monkish state but rather the marriage which He had created and instituted. He wanted His mother, although a virgin but not a nun, to be betrothed and a wife. Also, there is no doubt but that her caretaker, Joseph, although very chaste, was singularly blessed by the Holy Spirit. He didn't want Joseph to be a monk or some Essene but a husband, a householder, and the lawful husband of His virgin mother. Both of these were divinely-called to these very sacred ministries.

Christ wanted to be born not through marriage or as a result of marriage but not outside of marriage because, although his mother was a perpetual virgin, nevertheless she was a wife according to the Law and did not "know" a man according to the flesh. What greater praise could Matthew write about marriage? And yet, blinded as they are, they do not see this but something else, not something of the truth but from the doctrines of demons.

John the Baptist lived the celibate life as God called him into the wilderness to bear witness of the Light, but he himself never commanded celibacy to anyone nor did he forbid marriage, nor has anyone ever done this as a result of God and the truth. Montanist blasphemy first attempted this under the name of the Holy Spirit, as we read in Eusebius. Now through their coerced celibacy the Papists befoul everything with their lusts under the name of virginity and chastity. They cannot deny this. The situation itself cries out against heaven, etc.

"Before they came together, etc.," and a little later: "He did not 'know' her until she gave birth to her firstborn son." As Matthew looks back to the prophecy of Isaiah, he wants to say nothing else with these words but that a virgin conceived and gave birth. If she was pregnant and gives birth before she had sexual relations with a man, then surely she conceives as a virgin and bears a child as a virgin.

Helvidius, against whom Jerome wrote, argues foolishly from this that Mary later had relations with her husband and bore other children whom the Gospel calls "the brothers of the Lord," unaware as he was of the Scriptural phrasing which speaks in this way: "The raven did not return to the ark until the waters dried up," which does not mean that it returned later but rather that it never returned. Also: "The Lord said to my Lord: 'Sit at My right hand until I place your enemies under your footstool.'" Who would say that this means that, after the subjection of His enemies, Christ would be cast down from the right hand of the Father, that is, that He considered His enemies His footstool in such eminent fashion?

The foolish Helvidius was thinking that this pertained to the fact that Matthew is saying here that Christ is the firstborn of Mary. He is asking: "How can he call Him the firstborn after whom there followed no other to have the position of 'second born' or 'third born?' After all, if no brother follows, we are correct in calling him not the firstborn but the 'only begotten.'" But he is saying this out of his same foolish ignorance of Scripture.

According to the Law, when her firstborn opens the womb of his mother, she must offer him to God on the fortieth day from his birth. Within that time, other children cannot be born to that woman to be called the "second born," "third born," or "fourth born." Otherwise the Law would be impossible, for I would have to offer the firstborn on the fortieth day, and I do not know whether he is the firstborn. If, however, I wait until the women bears more children because of whom that first one was truly the firstborn, the time passes which the Law prescribes, and I become disobedient to the Law. Furthermore, we are sure that in Scripture that child is and is said to be born first, whether someone or no one follows. If, then, no one follows, that same child can be the firstborn and the only begotten, just as all people understand. The fanatic spirits, however, as they now are, have always been eager to busy others with vain thoughts to turn them away from necessary ones and from the article of justification.

Mary was found and detected to be pregnant. Because she was betrothed, therefore others suspected nothing evil. Joseph, however, was burdened with suspicion because he had not touched her; but the angel described all these things in such a way that we see this virgin mother just as Matthew says: "All these things happened that…" Also, Luke says that Mary was a virgin before she was publicly betrothed to Joseph, so that God sent the angel Gabriel to tell that this virgin was going to be the mother of Christ through the Holy Spirit.

But why does Matthew call Joseph "a just man?" Was it because he was unwilling to make Mary defend herself before the judges but was willing to divorce her secretly? I respond. Although on the basis of the Law he could have brought charges against her, nevertheless he kept hidden what he did not understand, provided this did not make him a participant in criminal activity, if there were any. This is the righteousness of the just over against the righteousness of the scribes and Pharisees, namely, not to pursue their rights because of their love, as you will see later from the teaching of Christ (Mat. 5), that you know how not to pursue all things even with the highest right to do so. Let us disregard our right toward our neighbor when we are with him on the way, for God also disregards His right toward us by making us blessed people through grace from being malefactors. Furthermore, we should conceal the crime of a brother, which perhaps is not a crime but merely a suspicion.

There was an unnatural uprightness and decency of behavior in the Virgin Mary. She would allow nothing improper to be suspected of her, and yet, what should a person think when he sees the indubitable signs that she has conceived? Therefore, God quickly discloses through an angel the mystery of which her husband was ignorant. The angel calls Joseph "son of David" to remind him of the promise made to David concerning Christ. The angel also adds: "Don't be afraid, etc.," that we may know that we must not hold in contempt our suspicion. You see, this just man would not have dared to live together with her because of his conscience toward God.

When you read here that the angel of the Lord appeared to Joseph in or through a dream, and similarly, in the following chapter that an angel appeared to the magi and to Joseph again, you are correct in asking whether we must believe dreams. I respond. When there is nothing else but a dream, we must not believe them because they have nothing certain and those images which appear therein are most confused. They happen usually as a result of our emotions, just as Cato says: "don't concern yourself with dreams, for the human mind desires something." The poet says in *Buco*[8]: "Those who love themselves invent dreams for themselves." In his book *de somno et vigilia*, Aristotle doesn't think that God sends people dreams and that other living creatures also dream. However, Cicero in his book *de divinatione* describes neatly that dreams of the more sober people are absolutely not empty but are often revelations of hidden matters as well as of future events.

With reference to dreams, whether empty or not, we assert that we must not depend upon them, for all of them cause us either fear or hope, and yet they are uncertain. Do you nevertheless contend that someone should forbid them for natural reasons? After all, physicians also pass some judgments from the dreams of the sick as to how their bodies are affected.

Also, if the things which happen in dreams are revelations of hidden matters or of things which are going to happen for our consolation or for us to be careful of some evil (for they also happen to Gentiles), let us acknowledge them as a gift of God, who is taking care of people. Then they know these things with certainty and

---

8    That is, Virgil (70–19 B.C.), *Bucolicorum Eclogae Decem*. viii.

have no doubts as to why they are revealed. Also, they cannot and should not determine anything certain from it with reference to the dreams of others.

In fact, we read that true dreams have deceived some people as, when Hamilcar[9], the commander of the Carthaginians, besieged Syracuse, he rejoiced to see [in a dream] that he was going to be the victor, although he nevertheless was taken prisoner there. (See Vale, 51.1, and Cicero.)

Scripture, however, forbids us to permit ourselves to be led away by dreams, either seen or imagined, as if by a prophet from the Word and the true worship of God which the Word prescribes (Deu. 13), something which wicked teachers are in the habit of attempting by imitation of true prophets to whom God used to speak in dreams. For this reason, I now shall tell what wickedness you see in Jer. 23: "They say: 'I have dreamed. I have dreamed, etc.'" The devil can send into us true dreams, something which they assert about the dream of Pilate's wife.

However, this was not the place for speaking about dreams except because of the opportunity, for Matthew is speaking not only about a dream, but also the angel of the Lord appeared to Joseph through a dream, and that Joseph entertained no doubt but that it was the angel of the Lord or that he spoke the word of the Lord. Accordingly, when he woke, he did what the angel commanded him.

If, then, you ask what those divine revelations are about which there is no doubt to whom something is being revealed, the answer is an easy one. It is wicked to not believe in such dreams. God speaks about the means of revealing in Num. 12: "If someone has been a prophet of the Lord among you, I shall appear to him in a vision, or I shall speak to him through a dream." Joel prophesies

---

9        Hamilcar Barca (275–228 B.C.), father of Hannibal. The reference to "Vale" is to a work by a first century A.D. Roman historian, Valarius Maximus, *Factorum et Dictorum Memorabilium*, Book I.7, ext. 8, where this precise incident is recounted.

about the time of the New Testament, and Peter cites this in Acts 2: "Your sons and daughters will prophesy, and your young people will see visions, and your elders will dream dreams." Those to whom God has made such revelations know and do not doubt when they awake both the dream and the revelation or interpretation, as Daniel says, ch. 10: "There is need for understanding in a vision."

In the meantime, it sometimes happens that God reveals a vision to some and the understanding thereof to others, as you read about the dream of Nebuchadnezzar and of the pharaoh. There is no doubt but that He sometimes still reveals mysteries today, just as Prudentius sings in his hymn before he sleeps: "O what deep secrets Christ discloses for the upright to see in their sleep! How clear they are, and yet how silent they must be kept. How rarely is it the fault of behavior. The serene light does not shake him and teaches the things which are hidden."

This whole thing happened, namely, that Mary conceived by the Holy Spirit, unbeknownst to Joseph, who had not touched her, etc., that the prophecy of Isaiah might receive fulfillment. He had said: "Behold, a virgin will conceive, etc." Let us see this in the words of the angel. He says: "Joseph, Son of David," to advise him of the promise which said: "Hear, therefore, O house of David. The Lord Himself will give you a sign. Behold, a virgin will conceive, etc." Also, Luke records the angel's words to Mary: "And the Lord God will give Him the throne of His father David, and He will rule over the house of David forever. Of His kingdom there will be no end." Obviously, he is looking back to that statement of Isaiah (ch. 10) about the baby: "Unto us a Child is Born; and unto us a Son is given. There will be no end of peace in the dominion of David and upon His throne to strengthen and establish it in judgment and righteousness now and forever." To these words, look back at the psalm about Christ which begins: "Give the king Thy judgments, O God." [Psa. 72]

Observing these prophecies at that time were the godly among the Jews and those, as Luke says (ch. 2), who were awaiting the redemption, one of whom was Zacharias, the father of John, who sang: "Blessed be the Lord God of Israel, because He has visited and redeemed His people." They included also Anna herself and Simeon, etc., as well also as those who had gone before, about whom Christ said: "Many righteous kings and prophets wanted to see and hear the things which you have seen and heard, etc." They observed them especially when they saw that Herod was ruling and when they saw the weeks of Daniel demanding the coming of Christ. But they especially observed most diligently these prophecies which came from the family of David, because they knew that Christ was going to be born from it, as it was said. Although many of the wicked held those prophecies in contempt or lost hope in them, crushed as they were by their slavery under the foreigner Herod, who could not have been king under the Law as if the promise of God held no water, and although they had very high hopes through the Messiah and thought the worst because of Herod; nevertheless, the husband Joseph was undoubtedly filled with the Holy Spirit. How, then, could he have despised such promises and not have considered them with very deep reflection? Therefore, he could easily have accepted the admonition of the oracle of God and understood through the Holy Spirit this very sacred mystery.

However, this angel adds: "Don't be afraid to live together with Mary, who was betrothed to you as your wife and whom you have not touched. This is not the situation which you feared, but that which the Lord has promised your family, because, as He said, that which is in her is of the Holy Spirit. Moreover, she will give birth to a Son, etc." The Evangelist respected all these things when he said: "Now all this happened, etc."

Moreover, when you hear "the Son of Mary," you hear "true man." When you hear "conceived by the Holy Spirit and born of a virgin," you hear "pure and without sin." But when you hear "who saves from sins," you can understand only that this is the true God, which we advised earlier.

"Behold, a virgin will conceive, etc." "Behold" is a word of wonder, for the angel intended to say that this was a miracle or, as he does say, "a sign," to be given to the house of David by the Lord God. Later, wickedness and envy drove the Jews against Christ, the Lord of glory, whom God had promised their fathers. Those fathers did not bear such a clear witness and made the false charge that Isaiah said that Mary was an "*alma*," that is, "a young girl," and not "*bethula*" or "virgin." They therefore caused Christians to interpret incorrectly "*alma*," when Isaiah says only "a young girl" would conceive and bear a child, namely, from her husband, and that this was a sign that she was going to bear a son and not a daughter. However, this was a very unusual sign and not just an ordinary one which the Lord Himself was giving the house of David, after He had promised some very great sign, whether it came from heaven on high or from hell below; namely, that a young woman will conceive and bear a Son, if not at first, then second or third, even after she had given birth to daughters lest this promise lose such a beautiful interpretation because of Jewish envy.

Moreover, if you should ask whom they understand as this young woman, they answer: "The mother of Hezekiah." However, the prophet does not say this. How, then, will they make us sure that the prophet says this about that mother and not about any young woman? Let these shameless rascals tell by what name their falsehood dies when either his mother or the people call him "Emmanuel." Furthermore, it is a very gross lie that they say that the prophecy concerns Hezekiah, who was going to be conceived and born, because, when Isaiah foretold this, Hezekiah was just a little boy, ten or more years old, something we know very well from the sacred history of the Kings, Chronicles, and Isaiah. Isaiah speaks about King Ahaz, but Scripture does not say in what years he ruled, nor do we spend any time here. Moreover, Ahaz ruled only sixteen years, and immediately after his death, his son, Hezekiah, became king at the age of twenty-five. As you see, his father had begotten him nine years before he received the kingdom.

Who then, unless he be clearly a dumb animal, would not see that here nothing is being said to the king and ruler Ahaz or about Hezekiah and his mother? Moreover, just as you see their insanity here, so also you recognize that this is a blasphemous falsehood, however much they have imagined that some young woman had relations with her husband here, which is something that strengthens our faith rather than moves us away from it.

In Lyranus see the fiction of others about the wife of Isaiah; but where is that Emmanuel, who in ch. 8 is called "the Lord of the land of Judah," whose lord or king was never Isaiah nor his son?

However, let us speak about the word "alma," that you may see that those wretched people have lost their God as well as their conscience, for they are unwilling to know here their very language and grammar. What will they do to their seventy very learned men and interpreters who, before Christ was born and before those blasphemies developed, translated "alma" as "παρθένος," that is, "virgin," just as Matthew and Luke did later? This is as if to say that the Latin does not mean "virgin" when it speaks of a girl who has not yet had relations with a husband, or it is not a stone [lapis] when it says "rock" [saxum]; or that the German does not intend the same when it says "Eine reine Jungfrau" or "eine reine Magd." Or, as if all languages do not use synonyms or periphrases in place of these. Thus, the Jews are laughing at themselves when they say that this is not a virgin when one says "alma" and not "bethula," because both mean "virgin." It is interesting, however, that "bethula" signifies a virgin regardless of her age, but "alma" signifies only a young virgin who is being kept for her future husband, whom her parents are rearing very decently and whom very honorable men can solicit for marriage. To the Hebrews "*alma*" sounds as if you be saying "hidden, protected and taught by here decent parents," because "*alam*" means to the Hebrews "to lie hidden, to hide or be concealed."

When the Holy Spirit wanted to say that a virgin would conceive and bear a child, and although He knew well that the Jews to whom He was speaking had two words with which to signify "virgin," He was unwilling to say "*bethula*" that no one might understand also an old virgin, and that the Jews who were of the lineage of David not compel many girls to remain virgins without marriage, which would be contrary to the Law, just as the doctrines of demons do waiting for the greatest old age until the Messiah should come from their own daughter. Who does not see how many secret fornications and how many mistakes have been produced through children born therefrom from the cloisters either of vestal virgins among the Gentiles or from monasteries among our people?

Rather, the Holy Spirit wanted to say "*alma*," that is, a young virgin, of marriageable age, beautiful, reared very honorably and highly commended by all, because of which her husband would be called "fortunate" to have taken such a girl as his wife, about whom not age, nor rearing, nor decency would permit anyone to consider her suspect of evil, such as was the mother of Christ, the Virgin Mary, when she was betrothed to Joseph. Thus, a virgin whom all had commended is handed over in marriage, and her husband keeps her without touching her, knowing as he does the plan of God. As a result, we never read that this mother to whom the Jews wanted very bad things to happen because of her Son heard anything bad among them. Her reputation was of such high integrity that they didn't even dare to tell lies against her despite their great envy.

Furthermore, that we may interrupt the Jews, they can produce for us from Holy Writ no girl who is called "*alma*" and is not a virgin. In Gen. 24, Rebecca, who was going to be the wife of Isaac, is called a "virgin," when Moses says: "The girl who went down to draw water..." "Girl" here is "*alma*" in the Hebrew. A little earlier he had said about this Rebecca: "She was very fair, namely, a '*bethula*,'" that is a very pretty girl who had had no relations with a man. In Exo. 2, the sister of Moses is called an "*alma*": "The '*alma* (we read "girl.")' went and called her mother." Why, then, was this "*alma*" not a virgin, about whom Isaiah said that she is going to give birth to Emmanuel, God, the Father of the coming age, the eternal King on the throne of David?

Go now, you Jew, and teach the Holy Spirit with what words He ought to speak about the honorable mother of the Messiah, that you now be forced to believe that you are waiting in vain for the Messiah after the weeks of Daniel and now over fifteen hundred years! Where is the Bethlehem in which Micah foretold the Messiah would be born? Where are the temple and Jerusalem where He is going to go, according to Malachi? Where is your priesthood and prophecy and kingdom? Where are all your sacred rituals?

You say: "The Messiah has not come because of our sins." However, God promised that the Messiah would come at a specific time without the addition of a condition whether or not you be sinners. Thus the prophets foretold that He would come for sinners and for the sake of sinners. Also, read Isa. 53. But can the God (who cannot deny Himself) become a liar because of your sins?

But what is your sin about which you are speaking? You are not worshipping Baal and other external idols; you are not killing the sacred prophets (whom you do not have) as you did before the Babylonian Captivity in which nevertheless God did not abandon you but gave you outstanding prophets and promised an end of the captivity after seventy years. Rather, you now have reached pure despair after so long a time. If, then, you think it true that the Messiah did not come because you were sinners, those sins must be greater than those most terrible ones which your fathers once committed.

Know then that your sins are not delaying the coming of the Messiah but that these are your real sins, namely, that you despised the Messiah when He came, that you killed Him, and that in your synagogues you are still blinded by terrible blasphemies, are still wicked and condemned, not just before God but even before the whole world. After all, who does not see that you are a cursed people? You have no salvation unless you accept by faith Him who you crucified.

Furthermore, I ask, from what genus or stem are you now awaiting that Messiah of yours? Tell me without lying, without hesitating and a bad conscience, who of you are of the house and family of David? Who of you are of the tribe of Aaron, that you may again receive the kingdom and priesthood? After the Babylonian Captivity, your leadership removed some of you from the priesthood because they could not prove their genus, that is, they could not declare with certainty that they were of the priestly class, and yet at the same time, they had been preserved for only seventy years in Babylon. Why do you think that there is such great confusion among the Jews who have now been scattered throughout the world for fifteen hundred years? They are only babbling and dreaming that among themselves there is one from Joseph, another from Levi, another from Judah; this one from the house of Aaron, and that from the house of David.

Thus, those who now are called Jews no longer know whether they are Jews or proselytes. That is, they don't know who among them are from the Gentiles, except from the fact that they obviously have received circumcision. You see, they are completely ignorant and cannot assert except with an erring or evil conscience that they are the seed of Abraham and children of Isaac and Jacob according to the flesh or even if they are born of the blood of the Jews. Especially, we don't know whether some are of the blood of Abraham nor can we ourselves assert with certainty that this or that person is of the blood of Abraham, because such confusion has happened to them.

Or are you ignorant of the account of the destruction of the Jews which occurred at the hands of Titus and which the Jew Josephus has described? Then, by the judgment of God, they all perished (as Christ had foretold), because they had not known the time of their visitation. The plague killed some, sedition and the sword slew others. Some the Romans sent into the provinces that the Romans in their games might throw them to the wild animals to be torn to pieces. The rest were sold to Gentiles and were surrendered into a terrible slavery. In the meantime, what did the Roman soldiers, who were wicked Gentiles, do with the girls and married women whom neither famine nor the sword killed? They sold many, certainly not to Jews but to Gentiles. The Jews were not from Judah and were not the children of Abraham. Rather, they were "goyim," that is, born of Gentiles. Furthermore, if the Jews who had been sold begot any sons either from Jewish women if they had any or from Gentile; oppressed as they were by their slavery to Gentiles, nevertheless they were unable to preserve their tribal unities and Jewish bloodline, for they had been compelled to suffer such great adulteries of the *goyim*, that is, of the nations, that they became useless slaves. In this way, no one was certain after so long a time a thousand years ago whether he was born of the fornication of the blood of Abraham or of that of *goyim*, that is, of sundry nations.

As a result, who does not see that it can happen that all these fools who were boasting about Abraham who are now blaspheming Christ, the Lord of glory, are not of Abraham according to the flesh but of shameful fornication with *goyim*? It thus happened by the judgment of God that, when they curse the *goyim* (that is, the nations) in their synagogues and suppers, they are cursing themselves, something which nevertheless happens because of these words:"They themselves will curse, but you will bless"?

I am saying these things not so much to revile with curses but to indicate how those who were unwilling to welcome the
Savior perished because of the horrifying judgment of God. Just
as their shrines were destroyed in such a way that no stone rested
upon another stone, so also God so degraded the blood of Abraham
that now no one could ever recognize it, just as the holy prophets had foretold. Those deplorable dregs therefore await uselessly
the Messiah. However, what will He whom they imagine to be the
Messiah, born of a man and a woman just as other people are born,
do to them?

But let us return to the word "*alma.*" When the blaspheming Jews see that they cannot stand against certain Scriptures, they
begin to seek other passages of Scripture which they can twist this
way and that with their invented interpretations in order to confuse
the unlearned on the basis of obscure and uncertain passages about
the very certain ones which we have cited and which are not obscure
in this matter. With their scoffing by twisting and perverting them,
they snatch them away into foreign and unworthy meanings.

They have only one passage of this kind (namely, Pro. 30),
where we read: "There are three things which are unforgettable to
me and, in fact, four of which I am ignorant: the way of an eagle
in the sky, the way of a serpent on a stone, the way of a ship in the
midst of the sea, and the way of a man with an *alma* - a virgin. Such
is the way of an adulterous woman. She eats, wipes her mouth and
says: 'I have done no evil.'"

Here they very shamefully explain "the way of a man with
an '*alma*,'" as a reference to sexual intercourse that they be permitted
to blaspheme although "the way of a man" never in all of Holy Writ
means this, and that they may triumph. Otherwise, as they say,
why would the author immediately mention an adulterous woman?
When some of our people wished to write against the Jews, they
there gave the Jews a handle for blaspheming with inappropriate

allegories which they imagine here about Christ and in which they abandon the grammatical and true sense of the words. See this in the explanation of Lyranus, that I not be wasting my time.

The meaning is this. Just as I do not know the way of an eagle in the sky and the way of a serpent upon a rock and of a ship in the midst of the sea, so also all the more ignorant am I of the way of some man toward an *"alma,"* that is, an adolescent virgin. This 'way of a man' is not corrupt intercourse, for we can detect signs of this. Rather, it is the love of a man who is soliciting a lovely virgin and struggling with that emotion which one cannot reach without pondering and without words. Although he who has experienced this cannot know or say sufficiently later how he felt toward the virgin, meanwhile, in all the things which he does; he thinks, speaks, and dreams about his beloved, just as we say about such a fellow. The entire matter is in the bride's hands, just as the poet says:"Now for a long time his mind has been in the stew pots!"[10] We read about this emotion by translation in the Psalm:"The king will desire your beauty greatly." The bride sings in her songs:"I am faint with love."

It is not at all common in Scripture for"way," when the subject concerns a person, to mean affection, manner, behavior, life, actions, teaching, scruples, etc., according to the words to which it is added, as in Psa. 1:"The way of sinners,""the way of the ungodly," "the way of the righteous." For this reason, you often read"the good way" and"the evil way" in Proverbs and almost everywhere in Scripture. Luther interprets this a little differently in his *vom Schem Hamphoras.* So why do we interpret here"the way of a man" contrary to the custom of Scripture so that we later are forced to say that"*alma*" means what it never means in Scripture?

What he adds in the fifth place about an adulterous woman he is not comparing or saying is similar to an adulterous girl, as people interpret this in a corrupt way. Rather, he is comparing sim-

---

10    The quote is from the comedies of Terence (195–159 B.C.).

ply and obviously the way of an adulterous woman which we have not yet understood in adultery. She rather deceives with her skill and cannot deny her way with the way of a man seeking to marry a young girl who is a virgin. There is no comparison to anything else than that this way is unknown for this reason, just as (as he says) he also doesn't know the way of an eagle, or a serpent, or a ship.

In this way, the way or emotion of a man toward an adolescent virgin who does not know what he is doing nor how the woman is affected has forgotten the covenant of his God, and no one can bear witness against that way or affection. You see, Solomon is saying this not about any adulterous woman but about a woman who is an adulteress secretly, for she says: "I have not done evil." Therefore, the suspicious Jews used to have a very harsh law of jealousy against wives whom they suspected [of adultery], as we read in Num. 5.

Here [in Proverbs] he is not comparing shameful things but rather five things which he doesn't know. He is saying this: "Just as others don't know the love of an honorable man toward a virgin whom he is seeking as his wife, and yet the man is a true lover, so also he doesn't know the shamefulness of an undetected adulteress, and yet she is a true adulteress." This is what a wise man wonders at. We see people who are good and evil, and yet we don't know what is within them, according to the words of 1 Sam. 15: "A man sees the things which are visible, but God looks upon the heart." There is nothing in this passage therefore which would compel fools to make out of "alma" a corrupt woman, which it never signifies in Scripture.

"Almoth" or "alamoth" in Song of Songs, therefore, signify the royal virgins who have to do with royal pomp and the glory of the court. Whether they want to or not, those unlearned who are the dregs of the Jews declare with utmost certainty on the basis of the same Song of Songs "almoth" means "virgins." In the sixth chapter, we read the following: "There are sixty queens and eighty concubines and *'almoth,'"* that is, young women, but not a number. In the Song of Songs, the Jews confess correctly that nothing shameful is being described but that this song is a divine one which the Church has always held as being in Holy Writ.

Therefore, they should say here what the *"almoth"* are if they are not virgins, for they are neither queens nor concubines (which certainly are included in numbers), but there are also *"almoth"* (of whom there is no [stated] number). You should also remember that in Scripture concubines are wives but they are not mistresses, nor heirs along with their children. Rather, they receive gifts just as these German women of the nobility receive a dowry and other things, just as also reads of the law of the children of concubines of Abraham in Gen. 25. If, then, the *"almoth"* here are deflowered women, that is, not virgins, they are neither queens nor concubines along with whom they are praised as "beloved" and "beautiful." If only one is preferred ahead of all, although they all are beloved and beautiful, tell me, please, what is this except shameful prostitution? That you not drag this into the account of Solomon in 1 Kings 11, know that there we have no mention of wives among whom are those which the Law forbids because of their idolatry. Of adolescent young women or *"almoth,"* however, there is also no mention here.

However, the royal lover has expressed great praise for us, as does also the Holy Spirit, from whom Holy Scripture has come forth, as if He wished to commend to us the countless flock of harlots against the command of God: "Do not commit adultery," and against that law in Deu. 23: "No whore of the daughters of Israel nor whoremonger of the sons of Israel [shall enter the temple of the Lord]"; and Lev. 21: "A priest shall not marry a whore or a profane woman nor one whom another man has divorced… And if a priest's daughter be caught in sexual misconduct, let her be burned in the fire, for she has defamed the name of her father." Here the Holy

Spirit wants the home of the priest to be very honorable ahead of other homes. Here He does not only want the priest not to marry a harlot but also not even one who has been deflowered even if she have been a very honorable woman who suffered this against her will, nor a woman whom another man has divorced despite the fact that she had been faultless. In this spiritual Song of Solomon, a spiritual song, is the Spirit here commending to us flocks of adulteresses?

Therefore it is left for us that here "*almoth*" means "virgins" when they are neither queens nor concubines and they cannot be adulteresses. The "*almoth*" are in the royal retinue. In another spiritual song, namely in Psa. 45, the psalmist calls them "*bethuloth*" who belong to the king's retinue where we read that "the virgins come after the king's daughter," etc. Who would now wish to be better-informed about the word "*alma*"?

However, those who are more learned among the Jews know these things, namely, that the word "*alma*" means "virgin," but not an elderly virgin, just as we have said. However, some do not suffer such clear testimony and jeer as follows: "Let's accept that '*alma*' means 'virgin.' Nevertheless, not even you Christians can hold or defend from Isaiah that a virgin conceived and a virgin bore a son or that a virgin is said to have conceived and would bear a child. After all, we can understand the words of the prophet is this way: 'Behold, a virgin, that is, a girl who is now a virgin, will at some time conceive and bear a son after two, three or even ten years, namely, from her husband.'"

They obviously are awaiting an egregious savior conceived from an unclean seed and who cannot save his people from their sins as one who himself has been conceived in sin.

Here certainly, when they speak about the words of Isaiah, they ought not cite our texts nor the translation of the Gospel of Matthew which they see are not appropriate for their false charge. After all, the holy apostles often translated for us from the Hebrew, not the words but the senses of the words. That they might offend either a Jew or some other unbelieving person did not hold them back, for they knew with Paul, 1 Cor. 14: "Prophecies have been given not for unbelievers but for the believing."

Moreover, although this reviling of fools and sophist accusation are so well known that he becomes ridiculous who claims that we must refute them and not rather despise them and laugh at them; nevertheless, the Holy Spirit has spoken through the mouth of Isaiah about this "*alma*" and this conception and childbirth in such a way that not even ridiculous jeering can have a place. Isaiah reads the following way in the Hebrew: "Behold, a virgin becomes pregnant and gives birth to a Son, and she will give Him the name 'Emmanuel.'" Unhappy Jew, do you hear that a virgin is pregnant and bearing a child, a miracle which the prophet sees as present in spirit, so that your blasphemous mouth is shut up?

But even after all these things, the insane cry out against us and say: "Your Messiah was not called 'Immanuel,' but 'Jesus,' something which even you yourselves confess. The prophecy of Isaiah which says that His name will be called 'Emmanuel' therefore has nothing to do with Him." Again, this is either shameless ignorance or a wanton calumny, for they themselves in the manner of Scripture attribute even more names to one person than the proper ones. The Latins call them "praenomens," "cognomens," and "agnomens" because of a nature, virtue, event, or office which is being attributed and whatever is declared about someone among the people. The Hebrews and Holy Writ say with a single word the name or calling or appellation, as we read in Ecc. 7: "A good name is better than precious ointment." Thus Christ says: "Blessed are the peace-makers, because they will be called 'the children of God.'" In the meantime, nevertheless they are called "John," "Peter," "Anna," etc.

Shall I then not call him who has the name "Peter" and "Simon Bar Jonah" also "apostle"? In the same passage, Matthew did not fear to cite the prophet that Christ was going to be called "Emmanuel," and also tells that the angel commanded that He be called "Jesus." Similarly, Luke, too, in one and the same passage tells that the angel said to Mary: "And you will call His name 'Jesus,'" and nevertheless adds immediately: "He will be great and will be called 'the Son of the Most High.'"

Here let the stupid, little people demand that He whom we call 'Jesus' we ought not call 'the Son of God,' just as there He whom we call 'Emmanuel' may not be called 'Jesus,' and because He is called 'Jesus,' we ought not call Him 'Christ'; just as they again accuse Matthew, who said: "...of whom was born Jesus, who is called 'Christ.'" So also, we ought not call Him "Savior" nor "God" nor "Man" nor "Prophet," because His name is Jesus. This then happened by custom of Holy Writ, namely, that a person whose name is Nicholas we cannot call "Preacher" or "Consul" or "Tailor," and, in fact, not even "Human Being." Whoever (as the Hebrews say) says or calls him "Human Being" lies, because he is not "Human Being" but "Nicholas."

If they don't know these things, they are utterly stupid asses, but they cannot *not* know. Therefore, they are false accusers or liars from their father, the devil. Why don't they rather accuse their own prophets and Holy Scripture, which call or name the Messiah with many more names? Jacob calls Him "Shiloh" (Gen. 49). Therefore, according to them, Isaiah ought not have called Him "Emmanuel." And, after he called Him "Emmanuel," he ought not have said about Him: "His name will be called 'Wonderful,' 'Counselor,' 'Mighty God,' 'Eternal Father,' 'Prince of Peace.'" In ch. 23, Jeremiah says about Christ, the Son of David: "This is His name which they will call Him—'the Lord, our Righteousness.'"

As I have said, the name of the thing among the Hebrews is its reputation and whatever one can say or declare truly about a thing. They call a "false name" a false declaration or reputation about a thing, and an "evil name" an evil reputation. We pray in this way: "Father, may Your name be hallowed." Also, in the psalm: "In Your name, O God, save me"; that is: "Save me through the power and grace, which we declare and believe about You, that we may glory You the more." Also: "Deliver us for the sake of the glory of Your name, O Lord." In Rev. 3, it is said to the angel of the church at Sardis: "You have a name to live, and you are dead."

Therefore, when you read that Christ is to be called "the Son of God" or "God," as Jeremiah calls Him "Jehovah," we do not understand unreasonably that He is going to have only such a name, just as some could make the false charge contrary to Scriptural custom that a proper name has been imposed on Him by men. Rather, we understand that the Holy Spirit foretold this for people to believe, teach, and confess about Him what He truly is, and that we now acknowledge and preach Him of whom until now the world has been ignorant as God and man, the Word made flesh; that is, we are calling Him in truth "Emmanuel," that is, "God with us," "Jesus who is saving us from our sins and reconciling us to the Father," and who was condemning us through the Law when we were acknowledging no one else but one who was contrary and alien to us.

Also, God is still not a Father to anyone before He is called "the Son of a virgin," that is, before He is declared and acknowledged to be "the Son of God" and "God with us." The Law is a harsh teacher, but only until Christ came, as Paul says to the Galatians. So also, with reference to the other names of Christ, understand that we shall make known, declare, believe, and acknowledge that He is such a God.

Let the Jews now tell whom else they can show us whom we may so call; that is, whom people in the world proclaim just as the prophets foretold. When we call Him our "Savior," that is, when the faithful, both Jews and Gentiles, declare Him as such and believe that He does save us, why don't those dregs of the Jews abandon their terrible blasphemy and take up for their life the One whom the Father has sent, just as the Law had promised?

His mother, the Virgin, called Him first "Emmanuel," for this in Hebrew was who He was. Obviously the Virgin herself will call the name of her Son "Emmanuel," because she first knew that He was the incarnate Son of God as well as her own Son. She worshipped Him and rejoiced about this Glory and Salvation of people. Then the angel said to Mary: "You will call His name 'Jesus.'" What His mother first knew, both Jews and Gentiles later acknowledged and preached, as Isaiah also says, ch. 9: "He will be called 'Wonderful,' etc." In the meantime, when Matthew refers to this, he does not relate the words but the sense of the words of Isaiah: "His name will be called, etc.," as I have said and as all the Greek models have it steadfastly: "They will call His name 'Emmanuel.'"

Paul speaks about this mystery of our salvation (1 Tim. 3), but actually, the mystery is of His great godliness, for He was manifested in the flesh, justified in His Spirit, seen by the angels, preached to the Gentiles, believed in the world, and taken into glory.

Up to this time, we have been speaking against the blasphemy of the Jews in favor of the truthfulness of the words of Isaiah and of Matthew which exclude the father and mention only the mother of the Son, that it is necessary for her to be a virgin. Their words confirm the article of our faith by which we confess that Christ is the only Son of God, conceived by the Holy Spirit, born of the Virgin Mary to dwell among us, just as John said: "The Word became flesh and dwelt among us." We also confess that the true Jesus does save His people (that is, those who believe in Him) from their sins, by His conception and birth in the world (about which Jesus Paul says in 1 Cor. 15: "The second Man is heavenly, from heaven."). By that conception and birth, He sanctifies and reconciles to the Father we who were conceived and born in sin and condemned by our very origin from Adam, the first man from earth.

This truly is the situation because He is Emmanuel, that is, God with us, just as He is also declared throughout the world in the Church of the saints.

# COMMENTARY ON MATTHEW 2.

On the day of the Epiphany of the Lord, we have the custom of singing and reading from Isaiah: "Rise, shine, etc.," and from Psalms: "The kings of Tarshish, etc.," and the like, which the common folk believe are foretold only about the magi. Nevertheless, we must understand them to refer to all the nations who were going to be summoned to Christ, of whom the magi (along with their companions) were the first fruits after the Word had become flesh.

When the prophets prophesied to their own Jews about the coming salvation of the nations, they often express those nations by name who were their neighbors and very hostile that they might keep their own people from admiring them. Those prophets also predicted that those very savage and destructive enemies were going to be added to the people of God and glorify God. Therefore, they often expressed by name the Babylonians, Ethiopians, Syrians, Idumeans, Palestinians or Philistines, Moabites, Ammonites, Cedar or Ishmaelites, who are also the Agareni and now wish to be called "Saracens."

Therefore, let us speak here about the calling of the nations, the reminder of which we owe the nations with very great thanks to God for strengthening our faith from the Word of God. You see, when Luke speaks about the infancy of our Savior, he first describes the Jewish shepherds whom the revelation of the angel summoned to the manger of Christ, and the preaching which they did of Christ in Bethlehem and its environs. Then he describes the proclamation which the holy man Simeon and the prophetess Anna made in the temple of the people of Jerusalem. Moreover, Matthew also describes for us with this wondrous account the fact that we are the called nations.

First, let us be armed against the Jews and the disputations of Satan. You see, although the Jews had the oracles of God (something which Paul calls in Rom. 3 their "great prerogative"), nevertheless, the same oracles of God kept promising salvation to the nations also. This covenant of promises of salvation was common to both Jews and Gentiles as brothers and children of one Father. However, the former used to read that covenant as if they were present to it, as we read in Eph. 2. We, however, as if absent, were ignorant of it, although this belonged no less to the Gentiles than to the Jews. It was to be revealed in a time foreordained from eternity and then to be proclaimed in all the world.

Where were the Jews when God spoke to the serpent in Paradise? Did the woman's seed bruise your head? Was not the entire human race sold under sin already when it was under the serpent, that is, under the devil, who had the power over death? God promised to take this power away from the neck of all people through Christ, the woman's Seed. This He said to Abraham, who certainly was neither a Jew nor circumcised, nor did He say about Jews alone in Gen. 12: "I shall make you into a great nation, and in you will all the nations of the earth be blessed."

The holy prophets understood this and proclaimed often the coming blessing and salvation of the nations. The psalmist speaks in this way about Christ: "All kings will worship Him, and all nations will serve Him." Also: "Remember and turn to the Lord, all you lands of the earth, for the kingdom belongs to the Lord, and He holds dominion over the nations." Also: "Ask of Me, and I shall give you the nations as your inheritance and the ends of the earth as your possession."

We read in Isa. 11: "The nations will place their hopes on Him"; and ch. 49: "It is a small thing that you be My servant to raise up the tribes of Jacob and to convert the dregs of Israel. I have given you as a light to the Gentiles that you may be My salvation to the end of the earth." Also, ch. 54: "Sing praise, you barren woman, who bears no child, etc." And ch. 60: "The nations will walk in Your light, etc." Again, ch. 65: "Those have sought Me out who weren't asking for Me before, etc." In Hosea 1, we read: "And it will be in the place where it was said: 'You are not My people, and there you will be called, "The children of the living God."'" Also, read Paul's comments in Eph. 2. Here we say confidently with Paul, Rom. 3: "Is He the God only of the Jews and not also of the Gentiles?"

Second, when you hear and read "Gentiles," understand (something which the situation itself cries out) a wicked people, ignorant of God, without God, without Christ, without the Holy Spirit, as we read in Eph. 2, clearly, the people of the devil and condemned, to whom Paul said, 1 Cor. 12: "You know that you were Gentiles, carried away as you were to dumb idols."

Third, we therefore are certain that when you hear that the Gentiles were called and taken up by God, that He took them up by no merit of their own nor because of their good works but solely by His grace, who, as we read in Eph. 1: "…loved us in Christ before the creation of the world in praise of the glory of His grace by which He made us pleasing in His beloved Son, etc." Read also Rom. 9.

Fourth, we are also certain of this, namely, that God took up the Gentiles without the Law through faith. Here the Jews are so far from boasting against the Gentiles that they did not reach the law of righteousness by pursuing the law of righteousness, because they [the Jews] sought righteousness not from faith but only from the works of the Law as they stumbled against the stone of offense. The heathen, on the other hand, who were in no pursuit of righteousness, did lay hold of righteousness but only that righteousness which is of faith, as you read this in Rom. 9, which words Paul had to repeat about the rejection of the Jews and the election of the Gentiles; and in Mat. 8 in the account of the centurion. Thus you may now see in Rom. 3: "All, both Jews and Gentiles, have sinned and come short of the glory of God." Furthermore, "they are justified freely, through His grace, through the redemption which is in Christ Jesus, etc."

Never in eternity will there be another justification of sins before God, something which all consciences of the saints or of the justified confess along with us on the basis of the preaching of the Gospel or of grace as well as experience itself. In this way, "every mouth is shut, and all the world becomes subject to God, for no flesh will be justified in the presence of God by the works of the Law." If justification comes not from the works of the Law, all the less will it come from the works of human laws, about which the Lord says: "They are worshipping me in vain, as they teach the doctrines and mandates of man."

Fifth, you are asking how these magi became believers or how they arrived at faith. I respond: Just as we have, and just as Paul says, Rom. 10: "How will they believe in Him of whom they have not heard? Faith comes by hearing, and hearing by the Word of God." In some way different from public preaching, the Word and the goodwill of God toward them reached them. Nevertheless, on the basis of this account, the Word did reach them. You see, although they perhaps had from their fathers the Word about the coming Savior, and although they may have feared God as did Abimelech (Gen. 20 and Gen. 26), as well as Job; nevertheless, we cannot assert this with certainty.

However, we are certain of this, namely, that along with a star they had a revelation of the Word of God either vocal or inspired by a secret spirit. If not this, then that happened only from seeing the star. Although by this new and wondrous way they could not have known the King of the Jews had been born, as they confessed that they knew; much less could they have known that this King of the Jews had anything to do with them because they were not Jews but heathen, just as they confessed that they belonged to Him. They said: "We have come to worship Him." They therefore developed faith from the Word or from the revelation of God, and by the star as a sign and mystery of grace they received a strengthening in their faith, as we read: "When we saw the star, we rejoiced with very great joy." This is the joy of conscience in the Holy Spirit.

However, just as they believed, so also they confessed their faith even when there was danger for their life there, namely, in the royal city of Jerusalem, where King Herod lived and where it certainly was the crime of lese majesty to name someone else as king and wish to worship him. Paul says: "With the heart one believes for righteousness, and with the mouth one confesses for salvation."

Sixth, after these magi became godly from ungodly and believing from unbelieving, God now took them up and made them the children of God. See how they bore witness of their faith with a new life and declare by their very fruit that through the grace of God they have become good trees. Led as they were by the star and the revelation of God they came to the Baby Jesus. They took no offense at the contemptible and vile conditions, namely, the poverty and weakness of the infant, the very despicable squalor and filth of the stable or little room, although there was absolutely nothing which did not lead human reason to a great contempt. In this way you see that their faith was true, solid, and steadfast. They rather went straight ahead and worshipped the Baby. After all, true faith and confession cannot help but worship God and Christ the Lord. Therefore, that is worship even if you don't fall flat on your face. Acknowledge God as your Father in Christ and Christ as your righteousness, and in this way you truly worship.

They also offered the Baby gifts from their treasures— gold, frankincense, and myrrh, as they considered at the same time both the poverty and odor of the place. Thus I need not say or repeat anything else any longer about those things which people are in the habit of saying about these gifts. Christ always receives the good works or benefits of His faithful people which they give up for their needy neighbors as gifts and, in fact, as sacrifices given to Him, for He says: "What you have done for one of the least of those who belong to Me you have done for Me. I was hungry, and you gave Me something to eat, etc."

You also see next that they believed the Word of God and loved the Word, because they believed the oracle of God which they later received in their sleep, when Christ said contrary things about some who believe for a time and in time of temptation turn away.

They are offended because they see everything despicable there. For instance, they see that none of the Jews are seeking the King who was born for them, and they see that Herod is setting snares for those who are seeking Christ. They nevertheless remain steadfast in their faith according to those words of the psalm: "There is much peace for those who love Your Law." They take no offence at these things; that is, no power of the world and no fruitlessness of it misleads them from the Law, that is, from the Word of God. That's how far they were from being offended and from recoiling at the weakness of their brothers.

But now, these magi who had experienced conversion to Christ did not now think up some superstitious kind of life nor did they abandon their calling which was to be useful to others, as the Papist crowd does in the case of their monks and as the Anabaptists do today. Rather, accepting the admonition of the Word, they returned to their own country and therefore were forbidden to remain in Bethlehem or elsewhere in Judea. I have no doubt but that those wise men served the state in their own area. Did they leave the office of serving others and imagine that they were leaving the world, just as lazy people without faith do among us under the guise of worshipping Christ, contrary to the Word and will of God and contrary to the reckoning of sound faith, when, on the other hand, God wants us to serve others? For the sake of Christ and because you have become a Christian, there is no need for you to change your calling, as Paul writes (1 Cor. 7).

Thus, after a revelation from heaven led the shepherds (about whom Luke wrote) to Christ and after God had honored them so highly in this way, they did not despise this as some new religion but felt that the true and only religion was to believe in Him whom heaven had revealed to them. They made known publicly and confidently that Christ became incarnate for us, so that they were surprised at how many listened to them. This is their confession of their faith. They returned to their own flocks and kept their own calling, content as they were with their own lot, until God wanted or gave better things, just as Paul says: "If you can be free, use the better thing."

In their insanity, the Anabaptists make people in this life and political activity equals and are unwilling that servants be obedient—but you see the contrary in these shepherds. They don't lack masters who have control, the contrary of which you see in these magi. Whoever there is here, whether he be Jew or Gentile, whether he be master or servant, he returns to his own vocation.

In the meantime, however, this is true. After conversion (that is, after you have believed in God through Christ), you must not return to unbelief, to idolatry, to condemned errors, to blasphemy, to disobedience, to shameful crimes. Otherwise, what would your conversion be which is rather a turning away from God? Or where would faith be staying in such things? We must not deny penitence to those who have fallen, nor must we think that a person can be perfect and without sin in this life. Rather, a Christian does not love his frailty nor does he commend his errors and sins. He always trusts in the mercy of God and believes with certainty the forgiveness of his sins. This Matthew has expressed about those blessed magi in the fact that the oracle of God admonished them not to return to Herod, that is, to a wickedness which would destroy them.

Meanwhile, I am saying these things that no one think that these good trees, namely, the heathen who have been called to the faith, do not produce good fruits, that is, good works. But good works do not justify them before God; rather, when they become children of God, justified as they are by faith, those very works are justified so that they are just and good works. You see, the person becomes pleasing through faith in Christ, and his works become pleasing because of the person who does them. Otherwise, whatever is not of faith is sin. The works of those who are the justified children of God are righteousness, which does not justify before God but which is justified by God and made acceptable because of the children of God who perform them. Such works sometimes even have their own promises of grace, about which we shall speak elsewhere.

Up to this point we have been saying these things about the faith and calling of the heathen and about the good works of believers. For the remaining points which have to do with this, see our *postilla*.

"When Jesus was born..." This is the joyful Gospel, namely, that He, Jesus, whom the Law and the prophets had foretold, was born, that is, the Justifier (Rom. 3).

"...in the days of Herod, the king." Luke also arranges that in this way: "There was in the days of Herod the King, etc." The Evangelists are signifying that it was now the time for Christ to come, as they describe when a foreigner ruled in Judea through the power of the Romans according to the prophecy of Jacob in Gen. 49: "The scepter will not be taken from Judah, etc.," and of Isaiah, ch. 11: "A shoot will come forth from the root of Jesse, etc.," that is, from the nearly dead trunk of the propagated kingdom of David, etc. The seventy weeks of Daniel signify this time to us.

"…in Bethlehem of Judea." Just as he indicates the time of the birth of Christ, so also he indicates its place, which Micah had foretold (ch. 5). The heathen are seeking Christ, and the Jews are upset. As we have said, the prophets had predicted these things. Matthew signifies all these things that we may know that this is the Christ, conceived by the Holy Spirit and foretold by the prophets, etc.

"…wise men from the East." With respect to the people of Jerusalem, the Chaldeans and Syrians lie to the east. The magi (as the Greek philosophers call them) are summoned from there. They are teachers of the people, counselors of the kings or even priests, men of the highest authority, about whom Strabo says, Bk. 11: "The college of the Parthi was twofold: one of kin-by-marriage, the other of magi or wise men. Their kings came from both groups."

"…came to Jerusalem," as if so great a king as they were seeking had to be born only in the royal city and the largest city of the entire kingdom. This is the sort of judgment the flesh without the Word of God makes about the Church so that the Church is where the flesh sees the parade of ceremonies and the splendor of worship.

But the Holy Spirit knows this as an article of faith: "I believe in the holy catholic Church." You need faith to recognize the holy Church, for you see her face where the Gospel is proclaimed and the Sacraments of Christ are administered correctly according to the institution of Christ, although the rest of the things may appear contemptible.

Christ is born not in glorious Jerusalem, but in contemptible Bethlehem; not in the royal court, but in a stable. He is revealed not to the arrogant and wise, but to infants, namely shepherds; not to little old saints who are presumptuous in their own righteousness, but to sinners, namely, to heathen magi. Do you want to know where the Church is in which Christ is until the end of the age? Don't ask human reason, which looks to pompous surface appearances, but ask the Word of God. Here reason dreams that Christ was born in Jerusalem, and that's where the magi come. The Word of God according to Micah says that Bethlehem is the place of His birth. Without the Word all things are uncertain, however much they seem to have the reckoning of wisdom. But the Word makes the conscience certain, illumines it with its truth, and gladdens it with its promise, just as happened here in the case of the magi.

After they had heard and believed the promise, they obeyed the Word and came to Bethlehem. The star which they had seen in the East again appeared, went ahead of them, and led them to Christ, etc.

"'Where, etc." This question is a fearless confession of the truth.

"Herod was troubled and all Jerusalem with him..." Unbelievers cannot rejoice over the coming of Christ and the preaching of the Gospel so that the thoughts are revealed from many hearts. The magi indicate the time. However, the priests of the Jews indicate the place, and in this way the Jews have no excuse.

"[Herod] asked strictly..." He omits nothing as he sets snares for Christ. However, as we read in Proverbs, ch. 21: "There is no wisdom nor understanding nor counsel against God." Here we should speak about the ill will of the human heart, but we shall do this elsewhere, perhaps when we speak about the beheading of John.

Herod says "the young child," for pride did not permit the king to speak precisely.

Read Micah 5, where the prophet says that this ruler from Bethlehem has been from eternity, that is, is God. What he says: "... for from you, etc." signifies that He was going to be born there but would not remain there, because He had to spread His kingdom also among the nations, just as there: "The Law will go out from

Zion, etc." And there: "The Lord will send out the rod of His power from Zion, etc."

With reference to the star, see my *postilla*. With reference to the Herods as also to the gifts, read the *Cario* of Philip [Melanchthon].[11] Others are of various value.

"[They were warned] by an oracle." This is the concern of God the Father concerning the faithful in any dangers, according to the psalm: "I am with you in tribulation, etc."; and Isa. 43: "Do not be afraid, for I have redeemed you and called you by your name. You belong to Me. When you pass through the waters, I shall be with you; and the rivers will not overwhelm you. When you walk through the fire, you will not suffer burns, and the flames will not burn against you, for I am the Lord, your God, the Holy One of Israel, your Savior."

But here you need faith, etc. In this way, God cared for the child Moses, who was exposed to the waters. In this way, He cared for David who was suffering the ambushes and persecution of Saul. In this way, He cared for Joseph when his brothers sold him, etc. God permits and does these things, and yet we do not believe.

"When they went away…" Matthew omits the material about the day of purification, when the people listened to the heavenly utterances of Simeon and Anna about the Child Jesus, who was offered at Jerusalem. The report of this was later divulged because neither the shepherds nor those who had heard it from them kept it silent. Herod became upset about all this. When he saw that the magi had tricked him, he began to rage against the little children of Bethlehem, as we read later. Thus Luke writes those things and, in the meantime, he omits those things which Matthew writes here about the slaying of the infants and about the flight of Christ into Egypt.

11    In 1532, Melanchthon published an edition of the *Chronicle* of Johann Cario (1499–1537). Cario's work was a history of the world. Cario served as court astrologer to Elector Joachim I Nestor of Brandenburg.

Therefore, what you read here (namely: "When they went away, behold, the angel of the Lord appeared, etc."), understand from Luke that this happened after the purification. And what Luke says, namely: "When they completed all things according to the Law of the Lord, they returned to Galilee to their own city of Nazareth," understand from Matthew that this happened seven years later. You see, in the meantime, after the purification, they went off into Egypt. They remained there until the death of Herod and later returned to Galilee, as Matthew also says later, in agreement with Luke.

"Flee into Egypt." Again, as we said about the magi before, you see here the paternal concern for His Son. This is what Christ Himself is saying in John when He testifies that His hour had not yet come. With this outstanding example, Matthew is teaching that God cares for us. Let us simply believe this thing and say with the psalm: "My times are in Your hands"; as if to say: "They are not in the hands of those who wish me evil." Also: "There are many who say to My soul: 'There is no salvation for it in God.' But You, O Lord, are my shield as You glorify me and lift up my head, etc."

However, when the hour which God has appointed for us to obtain our salvation has come, let us understand and be certain that we, as the children of God, are not suffering these inconveniences at the hand of an angry God but by the goodwill of our Father toward us; for "whom He loves, those He corrects, etc." Let us pray: "Father, if it can be done, take this cup away from me; but let not my will but Yours be done. Lead us not into temptation, but deliver us from evil. Were we to believe these things, nothing would be more blessed for us, whether prosperity or adversity attend us, etc."

Because Christ does flee here, you ask whether we are permitted to flee persecution, for it appears that we may do what Christ does. I respond. Either on the basis of this passage or from this action of Christ, you will not safely confirm your conscience that you may flee if you don't have a specific message about flight or if you don't know for certain that you are free to do this and not forbidden to do it.

First, you are not Christ, for He Himself knew His own time and hour, nor did He flee to escape. He rather waited for His own hour, which John says clearly, ch. 14: "Jesus, knowing that His hour had come to pass from this world to the Father..."; and ch. 18: "Jesus, knowing all things that were going to come upon Him, went forth and said to them: 'Whom are you seeking?'"

You see, there are some things which are personal, that is, some things which people do which are forbidden to others (I am not speaking here about miracles.), as that Christ threw the buyers and sellers out of the temple, that Elijah killed the false prophets and priests of Baal, that Gideon destroyed his adversaries, etc. These happenings nevertheless have their own commandments from God. Therefore, we cannot argue against them and say: "Christ did this, Elijah did this; Gideon did this. Therefore I shall do it, or I am permitted to do it." The government has permission to do many things because it has its power from God, but these are not permitted to the private citizen.

Next, you see there that Christ did not flee into Egypt on His own authority but on the authority and command of God, because the angel brought Joseph this message of God: "Get up and take the Child and His mother and flee into Egypt, and remain there until I command you to do something else." If you receive such a message about fleeing or some unique word is sent to you or revealed to you, there is no need for you to question whether or not you may flee; for through the Word of God even those things become sacred which otherwise are illicit and forbidden by law, such as robbing or cheating your neighbors, which this Law forbids: "You shall not steal." Furthermore, when the Lord said to the children of Israel: "Rob the Egyptians and cheat your neighboring Egyptians" (Exo. 11); not only were they permitted to do this, but they even had to commit fraud. By being obedient, they performed a good work which the Word of God made holy, although it otherwise was very wicked and worthy of the vengeance of God, as Paul says (1 The. 4).

This example of the fleeing Christ therefore does not resolve the question as to whether we may flee in persecution. He Himself did not abandon His calling nor truly flee His own persecution which He was going to suffer. Rather, because He knew all things, He kept Himself safe for His own time to save us.

Let us therefore ask the Word of God that we may be certain whether or not we may flee in the persecution of the Gospel. We have a sure Word of God that we have permission to run away in Mat. 10: "If you have been persecuted in this city, flee to another." Also: "If they do not welcome you, leave those homes or that city, shake off the dust from your feet, etc." Also: "Be as wise as serpents, and be careful of those people, for they will hand you over to the council, etc."

In his book about flight in persecution, Tertullian contends that the command of Christ ("Flee to another city") is only temporal and pertains solely to the apostles who were preaching in Judea before the passion of Christ, just as Christ also commands that in the same place: "Do not go off onto the road of the Gentiles, and do not enter the cities of the Samaritans, but go rather to the lost sheep of Israel." Later Christ said: "Go into all the world and preach the Gospel to every creature." So then (as Tertullian says) the exception of the way of the nations and the way into the cities of the Samaritans ceased. So why, then, did not the command to flee also cease?

We can respond to this that the Lord later said about the Gentiles: "Go to all nations." But we do not read that He removed the precept or permission to flee. It does not follow that He removed the one and therefore He also removed the other. After all, He published another command about the former but left the latter intact. Otherwise, if the argument of Tertullian is a valid one that if, after the sending of the Holy Spirit, the command to flee was annulled because the prohibition about going to the Gentiles had been removed; so also, the other things which were forbidden to the apostles were removed after the sending of the Holy Spirit: "Go forth, preach, saying that the kingdom of heaven is at hand. Heal the sick, etc." Christ says: "Behold I am sending you as sheep into the midst of the wolves, etc. When they have handed you over, don't be concerned how or what you should say, etc. Have no fear for yourselves at the hands of those who kill the body, etc." You see that all these things in the same context of the command of Christ are absurd.

If, on the other hand, you oppose to Tertullian that, after accepting the Holy Spirit Paul was let down in a basket and fled, and that his brothers aided him in his flight, but they were so far from rejoicing that they felt that they had sinned, as we read in 1 Cor. 12 and Acts 9; he responds: "But the same Paul in Acts 21 responds to his brothers who were weeping and questioning because of the prophecy of Agabus: 'Why are you crying and breaking my heart, for I am ready not only to be bound but even to die at Jerusalem for the name of the Lord Jesus.' And they said: 'May the will of the Lord be done.' Nor did they propose to Paul the command: 'Flee to another city,' for they knew that this had ceased."

In this way, Tertullian wanted to drive out a nail with another nail. However, it does follow from his words that, once one has received the Holy Spirit, he is not permitted to run away, and that command or permission has ceased. Paul therefore sinned by fleeing, and the other brothers sinned by letting him down in a basket, and those sinned who asked him not to go up to Jerusalem, for they knew that the command to flee had ceased.

However, Tertullian goes on and says: "If the Lord wanted this precept to flee to continue, the apostles sinned who did not care all the way to the point of fleeing at the end." This is looking for a problem where there is no problem, caviling and playing games but not speaking with certainty. He is saying: "The apostles suffered. They therefore did not flee"; although they nevertheless did both in their own time for the sake of Christ and His Church in a holy and absolutely correct way, and they did not know what he [Tertullian] imagined they knew, namely, that the command or permission to flee had ceased when they had received the Holy Spirit.

Are we unfamiliar with the account of the Acts of the Apostles where Luke writes: "...just as the Holy Spirit was obviously sent into the disciples of Christ."? I tarry not a moment over the Montanist 'Comforter' of Tertullian. Didn't those about whom Luke speaks in Acts 8 receive the Holy Spirit? Didn't that great persecution against the Church which was in Jerusalem and all had scattered throughout the regions of Judea and Samaria except the apostles happen after the slaying of Stephen? They receive from the Holy Spirit no accusation of having sinned by fleeing nor of deserting. In fact, on this occasion God sent the Gospel of His Son also to others, for among those was the deacon, Philip, who, as he preached Christ, so also worked by the miraculous power of the Holy Spirit.

As we also read in Acts 11, some went out to the Jews and others among the scattered Gentiles and went all the way to Antioch. Why didn't the "Spirit" of Tertullian persuade these that the command to flee ceased after the sending of the Holy Spirit? Didn't Paul and Barnabas flee from Iconium to the city of Licaonia when they realized they were going to be stoned? Didn't Paul go off to Derbe after being stoned at Lystra? See Acts 14. The same Paul along with his friend, Silas, did not have to flee by night from Thessalonica, and later his brothers didn't have to send him away alone from Berea (Acts 17), if the precept to flee had been removed and it was no longer permitted to flee after receiving the Holy Spirit.

Look at how they used all the help which God offered in the meantime, how Paul appealed to Caesar, just as he betrayed to the ruler the snares of the Jews through a lad, that he not be killed by the Jews. Isn't this fleeing and taking care by all means that you not be slain?

Therefore, the apostles didn't know that the command of Christ ("Flee to another city") had ceased. That you not say that the apostles sinned after receiving the Holy Spirit by fleeing, God with His Holy Spirit was present with those who fled and worked miracles so that that flight completed the course of their preaching which the Spirit had commanded them. They fled in their own time on behalf of Christ and His Church according to the word of Christ, and they suffered in their own time for Christ and His Church according to the word of Christ. Both commands pertained to them (Mat. 10), and they changed neither, nor that other one: "Shake the dust, etc.," as you see in Acts 13.

Let us also ask Christ Himself, who had said: "Flee to another city" whether this command or permission has ceased. He responds: "Not because I said so and later did not change it." Or did He not command His disciples after they had been given the Holy Spirit to flee when He said about the destruction of Jerusalem and the Jews which was going to come after forty years: "Then those who are in Judea will flee to the mountains, and those who are under a roof will not go down into the house to pick up a shirt. Woe to those who are with child and are nursing on that day, for clearly they will not be able to flee easily. Pray that your flight will not be in the winter nor on the Sabbath."?

Therefore, you have a sure Word of God about running away which God has confirmed with His powers and miracles, namely, that fleeing is not forbidden. Now, if it pleases you, add for the confirmation of this sure Word the example of the fleeing Christ and other saints, just as you have seen the example of the apostles. I flee evil miasmas, dung, the plague, fire, flood, and bloody beasts. I also flee famine, as did Abraham (Gen. 12); as did Isaac

(Gen. 26). Why not flee also the sword, as Christ did here, and as did Jacob (Gen. 28); as did Moses (Exo. 2); as did Elijah (1 Kin. 19); as did the hundred prophets whom Abdias hid under the persecution of Jezebel (1 Kin. 18); as did David, under the persecution of Saul, as did the holy man, Athanasius, in the history of the Church of Eusebius and in the *Tripartita*, which man God preserved for the Church against the Arians miraculously through flight?

However, Tertullian says: "Christ wants us to suffer, but fleeing is not suffering." Let him complain to Christ, who commanded His disciples to do both in Mat. 10. It is strange that it comes into his mind to separate fleeing in persecution from suffering, as if he alone suffers who offers his neck to the executioner, but as if he suffers nothing who flees when sought for death, and is cast away from his property and possessions, from his wife and children and from his duties into exile and is never safe, like David, Athanasius, etc.

He certainly is fleeing the persecutor, but he is not fleeing suffering and grief. Also, he is suffering those things for the sake of Christ and the Gospel. Were he to wish to deny their truthfulness, he would not need to suffer those things. He nevertheless does not flee in such a way that, if he not be permitted to escape, he wishes to deny his faith in Christ and the Word of truth because of some punishments or death. In that fear, he merely prays God to remove that cup from him and that he not be led into temptation but delivered from evil. This is truly being among those about whom Christ speaks in Mat. 5: "Blessed are you who suffer persecution for righteousness' sake, for the kingdom of heaven belongs to them. Blessed are you who, when people cast insults against you and persecute you and say all evil things against you falsely because of Me. Rejoice, etc."; and among those in Mat. 19 and Mark 10: "He who has left homes or brothers or sisters or wife or children or fields for My sake and for the sake of the Gospel will receive an hundredfold, now in this time, homes and brothers and sisters and mothers and children and fields with persecutions, and in the coming age, eternal life." He does not say that the person fleeing or deserting his family and possessions is without persecution, but He does promise persecution to the suffering person and that he is going to have enough despite losing everything and regardless of where he goes, for the earth and its fullness belongs to the Lord.

Finally, Tertullian, carried by the heat of his debating, reached the point that he claims that he who is afraid to suffer clearly is not and cannot be a Christian. However, he who is not afraid of suffering will surely be perfect in his love of God, for "perfect love casts out fear. Many therefore are called but few are chosen." The question here is not who is following the broad highway, but who is following the narrow lane. Well, so much for Tertullian.

These matters certainly incline toward the doctrines of demons which cause sins for us where there are no sins and which cause confidence where one must be fearful. What am I hearing? That he who is afraid to suffer, that is, who flees, even if he should believe in Christ and be unwilling to deny the Holy Gospel because of some disgrace, loss, or death, nevertheless cannot belong to Christ. Also: he who falls in such tribulations for the sake of Christ and suffers losses of possessions as well as exile and is never safe, is not one of the elect and does not walk through the narrow gate but through the broad one, through egregious pleasures, namely, those of the world. Also: such a person does not have a perfect love. If perfect love were present, he would have no fear, according to the words of John. Is this obviously the wonderful comfort for those who suffer exile for Christ's sake? Abraham feared that they would kill him because of his wife. Jacob was afraid and ran away, as did also Moses and Elijah and the hundred prophets. They obviously do not belong to God. Christ foretold about Peter: "When you become old, someone else will dress you and take you where you don't want to go." He therefore cannot belong to Him who suffered, that is, to Christ, because he is afraid to suffer. All the less does another belong to God who says: "My heart is troubled inside me, and fear of death has fallen upon me. Fear and trembling have come upon me, and darkness has overwhelmed me. And I said: 'Who will give me the wings to fly like a dove, and to fly away and rest?' Behold, I shall wander far away in my flight, and I shall remain in the wilderness. I shall wait for Him who saves me from fearfulness of spirit and from the storm."

A person certainly can fear to suffer and do this without sin, something which we see in Christ as He prays for the removal of the cup of death and yet who took on every weakness of ours without sin. Presuming spirits are in the habit of failing in the face of temptation and the cross, as did the denier Peter. Moreover, fearful people and those who despair of their power and thus commend themselves to the mercy of God, God comforts in their faith, as did the crucified Peter later.

We read that Tertullian was slain because of Christ. If this is true, I believe that at that time he felt some of his errors deeply but that by the mercy of God they were not counted against him, and that he himself did not recognize these perilous laws in his heart. Next, just as he abused many other passages of Scripture in his books, so also here he abused the words of John so that you see how careless they were immediately after the times of the apostles. Thus the books of those who wrote such books were preserved because such things were laughable to human reason. On the other hand, the writings of those who spoke against such things have been lost as useless.

In that passage, St. John spoke about the wrestling of faith in which there is a terrible fear even in the case of the saints so that they say: "O Lord, don't abandon me in my madness, etc." Peter also was afraid as he walked upon the sea when he saw the storm rising up. Also, Paul says, "Within are fears; outside are battles"; but why was he afraid after such great blessings? I am now not mentioning our Head, Christ the Lord, as He agonized in the garden. But He speaks only about our love for our neighbor and says that it is a perfect love, not by comparison with some less perfect love but because it is true love, so that the perfect love there in John signifies what Paul says about "an unfeigned love," which is nothing else but true love.

Such love has no fear; that is, no bad conscience. It is not ashamed before a neighbor over a wicked impulse, advice, or deed against a neighbor, nor does it neglect its duty concerning that neighbor, etc. This is the confidence of our glory toward our neighbor. Furthermore, in the sight of God no one is upright. If we have not done something, or have done something wicked against our neighbor, we pray for forgiveness from our neighbor and become reconciled with him; and before God we shelter ourselves with the Lord's Prayer that it be a perfect love, that is, the true love which secludes or sends away the fear about which we spoke, etc.

So far we have been speaking in sufficient detail from the Word of God about whether we are permitted to run away in time of persecution. I believe that at his time Tertullian had a just reason as to why he was unwilling that some flee, as when he doesn't want a bishop or deacons to abandon the Church, and I shall speak about these later. However, he ought not have dealt with the simple question whether a Christian may flee in persecution in a way contrary to Scripture or the truth. He does the same thing in his handling of a military siege, of veiling virgins, of his exhortation to chastity when he makes second marriages unclean and not equal to the first, etc.

But it is a very beautiful thing when the enemies of the truth bring forth Scripture against us that we ought not run away if we wish to be Christians. They grieve that we do not offer our heads to murderers and that they cannot kill us whenever they wish. This is just like the tale in which the wolf complains that people don't trust him and promises peaceful intentions with the shepherd if he sends away his dogs. That is how the Arians made their objections to St. Athanasius that he was not steadfast and fled, and yet they were sad because they were unable to kill him. Athanasius responded very neatly to them in his *hist. eccles tripart.*, Bk. 6, ch. 22: "The wolf teaches the sheep not to flee, just as wicked shepherds [or pastors] teach us that we should listen to them when they teach against the Word of Christ, who says: 'My sheep do not follow a stranger but run away from him because they are unfamiliar with strangers' voices.'"

The word of Christ in John 10 seems to be against all these things: "The hired man who is not the shepherd and does not own the sheep sees the wolf coming, abandons the sheep and runs away, and the wolf catches the sheep and scatters them. But the hired hand flees because he is a hired hand and the sheep are of no concern to him. The Good Shepherd, however, does not run away but gives up His life for His sheep." He leads them forth and brings them to the most healthful fodder, so far is he from abandoning them. See also 1 John 3: "As Christ gave up His life for us, so also we should give up our life for our brothers."

Earlier, on the basis of Scripture, we claimed that a Christian may flee and that we must not make it a sin on the basis of the flight alone if nothing else happened, the way Tertullian makes it a sin. It is well-known that we spoke only about an armed persecution at peril of our body when we flee and about using a good opportunity which God is offering to save ourselves when we are permitted. We must be careful not take up the sword by rash, human presumption as if we are going to be brave and steadfast in our confession of Christ and the truthfulness of the Gospel. Let it not happen to us what happened to the apostles when they became presumptuous and too confident of themselves when they said to Christ that they were ready to go with him into prison and death, and then not only ran away but offended and fell from faith. Peter, who was more confident than the rest, also denied with an oath that he would do what the rest were going to do even if their adversaries had burned them, as they did Peter.

Although those had sinned and fallen from the faith, Christ preserved them for the Church through flight, when He said to His persecutors: "If you are looking for Me, permit these to go away, and this will be glorified before My Father." He said: "I have not lost any of those whom You have given Me."

However, this example has nothing to do with the question we are treating. You have no permission to flee that you may deny Christ and fall from the faith because of persecution as those about whom Christ says: "Some believe for a time and in time of temptation depart." When we teach from the Word of God that fleeing is permitted, at the same time, we are sure that we are not teaching that you have permission to deny Christ or to flee in such a way that because of your flight the Gospel and salvation perish among the brothers, something which I am saying now.

Therefore, this is from the word of Christ when He speaks about shepherds. This is not that simple question whether a Christian may flee, which is the question we have been treating. It is rather another question, namely, whether the pastor (that is, a doctor of the Church or the preacher) may flee. We certainly have seen pastors flee, for all pastors about whom you read earlier fled and could flee without sin, as Christ bears witness with His own flight, although He is the Pastor of Pastors and Christ the Lord who has done no sin, nor is there any deceit in His mouth. Nevertheless, those pastors are not hired hands, but are said to be (and are) pastors. They fled not disobediently (as did Jonah) and did not abandon their calling, but rather that they not be killed but serve elsewhere with their preaching, or return conveniently when the situation permits. They are not abandoning their sheep (that is, the souls which they

have gained for Christ), but are admonishing them to remain steadfast in the grace of God which they have received, just as Paul did
in the Acts of the Apostles. The sheep received that true, good, and
unique Shepherd, Christ, through the ministry of those shepherds
who have been put to flight and sought for death.

Therefore it was the duty of those sheep to remain in the
word of salvation. Others who, in the meantime, despise the Word
when they are permitted to hear it, lose the Word through the persecution of tyrants, and this by the judgment of God, as Paul says to
the Jews: "It was necessary that this word of salvation be preached to
you first, but because you judged that you were unworthy of eternal
life; behold, we turned to the Gentiles; for the Lord gave us this
command that we be the light of the Gentiles, etc." Isaiah therefore
says to us: "Seek the Lord when you can find Him, and call upon
Him when He is near." We can find Him and He is near when He
is close to us with His preaching and His Word.

Thus, those have been cast out flee and suffer loss and exile because of the brothers because they are unwilling to deny the
Word which they preached to them, nor were they willing to cease
from this preaching so that they were caught, if God permitted
their adversaries to do this. Because of their weak faith, those who
fled feared both the cross and death, and yet they were unwilling to
fall away from Christ, their Life-Giver, and from the truth which
they had preached to their brothers. In this way, they were prepared
to glorify Christ and His Gospel, as Paul says, either through life or
through death. As we have said before, is not this giving up one's life
for the brothers, as John says in his [first] epistle?

I do not see how someone may die for his brothers in any
other way than there was danger of loss of the faith or salvation
of the brothers. For in this way Christ (whose example John cites)
died for the sake of the Gospel which He preached for our salvation. Otherwise, if the brothers are not in this danger, they rejoice

over my flight and give thanks to God for my preservation, just as they helped Paul and led him along when he was fleeing, and this not only once.

I certainly don't want to tarry any longer over brothers who wish me dead when they say that Christians should not flee. In the meantime, I say that you should not think that John feels that I must free a criminal or die for the money of someone else except by chance for the Word by which I am rebuking those who are causing the harm and loss of property for others.

Next, those who are fleeing the sword in this way for the sake of Christ and the Church and are suffering exile have been prepared to die for Christ and the Church if God wanted this and to stand firm and not flee if the brothers must die because of the wicked teaching of others. I shall speak about this immediately, but how will you be able to call such people "hired-hands"?

However, that you may understand the matter more clearly, let us interpret the word of Christ regarding the hired-hand and his flight. The hired-hand, so-called from "hire," does not look at the advantage of his lord nor at his own obedience but only at his hire, just as he cares nothing after he has performed the work which he hired out to do. Such is the man who serves the Church and in this seeks only riches, high offices, favors, tranquility, his own advantages and not the salvation of souls. In the meantime, when all things are peaceful, and when he himself preaches the Word of salvation sincerely, people do not see him as a hired-hand, but as a true shepherd—until he sees the wolf coming. Such hired-hands Christ also calls "thieves and highwaymen"; thieves, because they set snares among our people as if they [the thieves] are teaching the Word of truth; but highwaymen because they kill the souls of those whom they have misled and also stir up an external persecution by misleading the common folk, as formerly did the false prophets, pseudapostles, and now the Papists and other sects.

Christ speaks about these wolves, thieves, and highwaymen; that is, false preachers. He does not say that the sheep listened to them, but only that they come to steal, slay, and destroy. It is then, I say, that the shepherd reveals that he is a hired-hand, abandons the sheep, and runs away, while the wolf catches and scatters the sheep. These are the words of a parable and are not physical, something which ought to be very well-known to the reader from the words of the Evangelist and Christ.

From the beginning, our question concerned physical flight which even shepherds can do, not to abandon their sheep but that they may be saved for the sheep, as Christ Himself did not flee that the wolves might catch the sheep that is, that doctrines of demons not mislead them nor scatter them, that is, cut them into various sects so that they do not cling to Christ and associate with each other because of bad consciences and uncertain doctrines, but that they might remain gathered in the unity of faith and sound doctrine, just as Athanasius fled and served from exile all the sheep of Christ as he wrote and omitted nothing against the ungodly teaching of the Arians, and just as Paul did, who, although being absent, nevertheless acted and wrote against the pseudapostles who had misled the Galatians, Corinthians, and others, something which these men could not have done, had they immediately offered themselves to their adversaries to suffer death.

In this way, they served the sheep by not suffering death. That is, it didn't happen that no sheep of Christ remained even if they were killed by the sword of the persecutor because of Christ, as Christ says: "No one can snatch them from the hands of My Father nor from My hands."

No teacher of the Church, stirred by an armed band or by rebellion as he is, can go out to meet the tyrants so that the latter do not kill Christians lest you drag the parable to that point to which it does not pertain. Rather, the parable is advising teachers of the

Church not to deny Christ in a time of persecution, just as Christ in His flight to Egypt did not do this to keep Herod from killing the innocent children among whom he was seeking Christ.

This mercenary did not look at the sheep but at his wages when he saw the wolf, that is, the misleader and the people believing in the misleading or false teaching. That wolf could have done harm to his wage, that is, money, honor, favor, and convenience, that he not be completely cast away and perhaps even to enjoy the greater favor of people. He therefore "flees" not by changing his location, but by stopping his confession of the truth. He flees from the truth and from Christ. He keeps the truth silent that he not lose his possessions and be in danger. He permits the wolf, that is, the servants of the devil, to carry off the sheep with his corrupt teaching. They do not teach the doctrines of God, but of demons from that ancient misleading serpent, and in this way scatter the sheep.

But the hired-hand does still worse and denies the truthfulness of Christ. He begins to speak and teach what the wolf wants, and this for the sake of wages, just as a hired-hand looks at nothing except that his work is profitable and he doesn't care whether his lord profits so long as he receives his wages. Here the wolf slaughters and kills the sheep; that is, the sheep who are misled do not remain in their field nor do they hear the voice of the shepherd, just as a dead sheep is not a sheep.

Nothing can snatch a true sheep of Christ from the hands of Christ, as He Himself says, for the voice of Christ, his true Shepherd, can bring him back even after the greatest errors. Nevertheless, as regards the present misleading, the hired-hand is responsible for the souls of all who have been misled. Against this, Paul, who surely was no hired-hand, said, Acts 20: "I bear you witness today that I am clean of the blood of all, for I have not hesitated to announce to you the whole counsel of God." He is not speaking about physical blood. Such a slaughter of all the sheep and the destruction of souls does not happen when the sword of the persecutor kills only the bodies of Christians, unless you should wish to say that Christ did not remain Son of God when He was killed and that the holy martyrs did not remain the sheep or children of God when they suffered all the extreme torments for Christ, etc.

How many mercenaries we see today under the papacy, who indeed understand the truth of the Gospel but, fearing as they do for themselves and their possessions, remain misleaders!

Next, Christ opposes those whom He calls "mercenaries" to good shepherds. The prophets call "evil shepherds" those through whom a wicked people perish as a result of the judgment of God because those people did not receive a love of the truth. In Jer. 5, you read the following: "The prophets prophesy false things, and the priests applaud them with their hands, and My people have loved such things"; and in Isa. 30: "The people appeal to an angry God. They are lying children, children who are unwilling to hear the Law of God. They say to the seers: 'Don't see'; and to those who look ahead: 'Don't look ahead. Speak to us those things which are right. Speak to us pleasing things. See the mistakes for us. Get out of our road. Turn the path away from us. Let the Holy One of Israel leave us alone.'" In Jer. 23 and Eze. 33, we read: "Woe to the shepherds, etc." And in Eze. 33: "If I say to a wicked person: "Wicked fellow, you certainly are going to die. You have not spoken as a prophet that the wicked person may protect himself from his way, for the wicked man will himself die in his wickedness. I shall require his blood from your hand etc." And in Luke 19: "Why did you not loan out my money at interest?"

With reference to those hired hands and their flight, which is an ungodly denial of the truth and shameful betrayal of the sheep for the sake of wages, we do not need to present the question whether they may flee the sword. Those who love their wages like the whore did in Hosea 2 do not wait until the sword comes but immediately fail and do what the opponents of the truth want them to do. It happens that, by remaining in their place, they run away and abandon their sheep as you have seen from the examples earlier. After all, you cannot say that Christ abandoned and betrayed His sheep by fleeing, for He had come to give up His life for the sheep.

That statement of Christ ("The hired-hand flees") therefore is not from the parable. Here it is cited appropriately when one asks whether a Christian or even a pastor may flee in a bloody persecution. Because of our reverence for true Christians and good pastors (who surely aren't hired-hands), it was fitting in this case not to cite that or oppose it to the word of Christ: "Flee to another place," which He and His saints did. Too bad that the wicked and condemned flight of the hired-hands is so frequent! However, that flight which our question concerns, happens quite rarely.

Augustine nevertheless cites this statement about the mercenary in a letter to Bishop Honoratus which we now read as Epistle 108. However, he himself deals very carefully and saintly with the case whether ministers of the Church may flee in persecution.

That we may finally conclude, let us leave the mercenaries behind and speak on behalf of the consciences of good pastors, who can say with Paul: "I did not shrink from announcing to you all the counsel of God." Christ fled, but He did not abandon His sheep nor cause the wolf to catch and scatter them, but in His own time He gave up His life for them all. The saints also fled in their own time and saved themselves for the Church. They die for the Church in their own time, if Christ wants that. There is a time for fleeing and a time for dying, both for Christ and the Church, because they don't want to deny the Christ whom they have preached to the Church. We may discern both times easily.

If I am allowed to flee, and if it benefits the sheep nothing that I die (In fact, they pray God on my behalf and they want me to be safe, just as the Church prayed for Peter when he was imprisoned and rejoiced at his deliverance therefrom [Acts 12]); why may I not depart, a pastor along with Pastor Peter, in the name of the Lord?

If I am not allowed to flee, I do not want to deny Christ but even confess Him with my blood and death and receive glory along with Jacob in the name of the Lord, about whom he speaks in the same place.

Moreover, if I am able to flee and if, because of my flight, the souls of my brothers are going to perish, for I am unable to defend their bodies against tyrannical violence; as I said before, I shall stay and give up my life for my brothers in the name of the Lord just as I remain with my Church as the plague rages, just as I now preach the Gospel for the sake of my brothers and neighbors, as the psalm reads: "It holds me back not at all that they excommunicate me and seek to kill me," just as when I oppose myself to the sects of Satan on behalf of sound doctrine and the pure Gospel of Christ and suffer reproaches, losses, and perils for the sake of my brothers that they may receive salvation.

You have my way of thinking. If anything still seems somewhat unclear to you, it is to your advantage to see Augustine in the aforementioned letter, whose main points I shall list here.

First, he says that Christians may flee who are not pastors and who are leaving behind them no one who was committed to their care. If they all run away (who at that time had their names inscribed in their own Church), the pastors are staying in vain.

Next, according to the example of Paul, pastors have permission to flee if there is not a general persecution and they alone are being sought for death. In the meantime, there is another good pastor or other good pastors or some good men who are not being sought, and they shall take care of the Church which they must not abandon so that she lies open to the wolves. However, if there is a general persecution of all the preachers, and if a fear pervades that, if they all are slain, there will be none to advise the Church, it surely seems advisable and necessary that the Church send some away in flight for their safety. Then human reason should not censure some for preferring that they themselves be saved ahead of others, nor should arrogance distort this situation as if they be better than others who are saved and are going to be of a great benefit to the Church. In his prayer, Augustine persuades us to commit the matter to God and that the Church send some away and keep others by casting lots, according to the words of Pro. 18:"Lots settle disagreements and sets lines between the powerful."

"[And Joseph was there] until the death of Herod." Christ therefore remained in Egypt for seven years, for Herod ruled for thirty-seven years, as Josephus writes, Bk. 17, _antiq._, ch. 9. Christ however was born in the thirtieth year of his reign.

"He slew all the children, etc." Did those little ones have the Sacrament of circumcision, that God wants to be their God, as the Law reads (Gen. 17)? So where now is that concern of God for those who believed, about which we spoke before? God now is permitting Herod to rage; but He has defined here the condition of the Church or of Christians and has placed before our eyes an example which leaves the impression that God doesn't care about nor has a concern for His faithful people when they are rejected by the world, as Paul says, and when even God seems to have abandoned them, often as if they don't exist or as if they are nothing to Him. Thus it is as if the Church has perished, just as you see Abel whom his brother killed.

In the meantime, however, Christians are saved against all the gates of hell or in death. The flesh does not judge nor see that those boys are saved; and yet, were they to live afterwards, they perhaps would persecute and kill Christ and blaspheme against the Gospel so that others of His assembly perished. Is this not clearly being saved? They are now immortal and in the presence of God and among the names of those whom Herod slew on the pretext of killing Christ.

Let Anabaptist wickedness keep quiet. Christ took up the boys as His fellow-soldiers and they cannot help but excel before God with singular glory, for they are the people of the Messiah, having a covenant with God. In this way, the Church is saved when she suffers oppression and seems to be about to perish. No power nor wisdom up to this time could prevail against her, something which Christ said: "The gates of hell will not prevail against her."

Notice here also how carefully Matthew cites the passage from Jeremiah about these slain children what was first said about the Jews who were going to be led off into the Babylonian Captivity and how clearly he confesses the resurrection, because Jeremiah foretold that the children of Judah would be brought back into their own country. In the meantime, however, he signifies that that leading back was the final resurrection of those whom the Babylonians and famine had killed or at least of those who in danger sincerely returned to the Lord and who had desired and demanded pardon for their sin.

However, when those children whom Herod had killed despaired in the flesh of living again because (as he says) they no longer are, that is, they have died and perished so that their mother Rachel could not accept comfort; yet Matthew says about them that what Jeremiah had foretold about the children of Rachel (as I shall say later) was true, namely, that we Christians are certain that they are going to be redeemed and brought back into a final leading back or resurrection. They will rejoice along with us, giving thanks that God was very concerned about their salvation, especially at the time when their sins were obvious and they were being slain. Were we to know this, we would also know that psalm: "My times are in Your hands," as we said before; and that statement of Christ: "All the hairs of your head are numbered."

"After Herod died, etc." Because God can do all things, you ask why He commanded Christ to flee? Why does He command

Him to return? Why does He not compel Herod and the other adversaries to give in? Or why doesn't He kill them and meanwhile save His own in peace?

I respond. God has appointed a time for our suffering and a time for our glorification. In the meantime, He wants to keep us on earth in the kingdom of faith and in His Word alone, just as He commanded Christ to go away into Egypt and then return that He might blind the ungodly to our wretchedness and affliction and complete their sins, as it is written about the Amorites. These temptations exercise and increase our faith more and more until the day of the Lord. We read in the psalm: "You will see, that is, rejoice over it, when sinners perish."

"...[and go] into the land of Israel." For, according to the prophecies, it was there that He had to begin His kingdom, suffer, rise again, and give His Holy Spirit.

"... [Joseph] was afraid to go there." This is strengthening for the weak who back away because of their fear of danger when they do not trust that they are going to advance something by the preaching of the Gospel. Add these ideas to those things which we said earlier against Tertullian about flight in persecution.

I have spoken in detail about the four citations in this chapter which Matthew makes from Scripture against the calumniators in favor of the absolute truth in Jer. 31.

# COMMENTARY ON MATTHEW 3.

Having passed over the infancy of Christ about which Luke writes some details, the Evangelist Matthew hurries on to the publication of the actual good news [or Gospel] or to the manifestation of the kingdom of Christ, for this was his intention when he thought that he would not arrive at it in fitting order unless he should first show that Christ had come in the flesh.

He begins the preaching of the Gospel and the new testament of God, as do the other Evangelists, with the preaching of John the Baptist, because the prophets (such as Malachi and Isaiah) had foretold that he would come before Christ. The Evangelists knew well those prophecies that John the Baptist with his preaching of repentance and Baptism would prepare for the Lord the people to welcome Christ, about whom he testified that He was the Lamb of God, taking away the sins of the world, etc. This was something about which John's father had sung in Luke: "And you, child, will be called the prophet of the Most High, and you will go ahead, etc." In these words, Zacharias has described the function and business of all the preaching of Christ in a very fine way. The Evangelist John wrote: "He [the Baptist] came in witness, etc."

However, John preached in the wilderness according to the prophecy of Isaiah, and the people went out to him. He did not preach in the schools of the Jews nor in the temple of Jerusalem. He did not stand at the altar clothed in priestly pomp to sacrifice. Although he was born for that Levitic priesthood, nevertheless he went about in contemptible clothing. He also did not live nor eat from the tithes, nor was he enriched by the first fruits, as were and did the priests, so that the people shrank away from him as from someone overcome. Why? To show that he was teaching a righteousness different from that of the Law, namely, a righteousness which was bound to no time, place, persons, laws, and observances, to wit, Christ, the Righteousness of God, and the Blessing of all nations, about which God had promised Abraham: "In your seed will all the nations of the earth be blessed." As Christ says, "this kingdom does not come with observance." With reference to this, He Himself also said to the woman: "You will not worship the Father on the mountain nor in Jerusalem, etc."

With that very harsh life he did not want to establish monastic laws nor some order; much less did he want to establish holiness or merit before God with such an observance, so that I am not saying that this was ungodly. After all, when did he teach this to the people or to his disciples? The foolish crowd of monks thinks that John did all these things without a calling and without the Word of God and faith. This is much different from the reality of John, whom God had called to do these things; for the Holy Spirit had foretold that he would be in the wilderness where he would live in that way. When, however, he did not perform any miracles to confirm his teaching (as we read in John), this life and behavior of his stood in the eyes of the Jews who were wondering at such things and considering them as a unique holiness, in place of miracles, so that they suspected that he was the Christ. For this reason, they had no excuse for not believing in Him whom they believed to be the Most Holy One.

But what holy thing happened as a result of this life, food, and clothing of him who had been sanctified in the womb of his mother before all this had occurred? Christ is not holy to our hypocrites, for He was not going to become suspect because of the clothing and behavior of John. Briefly, these things have respect for nothing else but that people believe his testimony for which alone God called him. He did not come because of such clothing or food, as we read in John 1. He came in witness, etc. We say similar things about Simeon and Anna, about whom Luke writes, that their life was commended not so that from it the righteousness of the flesh or the hypocrisy which imitates all things without the faith of the saints is commended to us. Luke commends their life to us to prove their testimony about Christ to us, and that those have no excuse who consider Simeon and Anna as saints and yet do not believe their witness or preaching.

"Repent!" We are certain that the "repentance" which he speaks of here is what the common folk call "contrition." With reference to faith, he adds separately: "The kingdom of heaven has come near." We also read in Mark: "Repent, and believe the Gospel!" "Repent" is taken frequently in Scripture in this way, so that repentance is a displeasure about something which was pleasing before and sorrow over a sin, something which the reckoning of the word includes. In Greek this is "μετάνοια." God thus speaks as if with human emotion in Jer. 18: "If that people should have repented of that evil which I spoke against it, I shall also repent of that evil which I though to do to it... And if it should have evil, I shall repent over the good which I said I would do for it." We also read in Eze. 18: "If the wicked person should have repented of all the sins which he has committed, etc." Paul says in 2 Cor. 12: "[I fear that] when I come again, God will humble me, and I shall mourn for many of those who have sinned before and have not repented over their unclean fornications and shamelessness which they have committed." Also, Peter said to Simon Magus, Acts 8: "Repent of this wickedness of yours and ask God is perhaps He will forgive you this thought of your heart."

Up to this time, however, we have not been receiving this from the teaching of the Scholastics concerning the three parts of repentance: *contrition* because of which sins are forgiven; *confession* which they make the executioner of the conscience; and *satis-*

*faction* in which we were confident but kept on denying the blood of Christ and the mercy of God the Father. They made these very things our works, and they established the remission of sins in these three, although there nevertheless can be no remission if we receive something for our work, merit, and satisfaction. All those things belonged to us here, but where is faith here? The remission of sins belonged to them without faith.

If those common things were insufficient, we used to flee to papal indulgences, vows and monastic merits, long pilgrimages, the establishing of sacrifices, and the building of monasteries—all of which are nothing more than pure blasphemy, wickedness, error, and misleading if we believe that the remission of sins comes through Christ. This happened to us justly because we did not take up a love for the truth, and for that reason God sent us the effective error, as Paul foretold. Otherwise, reason itself would have said that there is no remission of debt when there is a demand for any kind of payment. We ought to have trembled at the Word of God, as the Lord Himself teaches (Isa. 66). Because of our contempt for the Word of God, however, we learned to tremble at the word of men who kept commanding us to do what God did not command, of people who imagined righteousness from our own work as if from the Word of God.

How strange it is that we trembled at the name of Augustine. However, Augustine is not at fault for this, for he clearly advised that we not take up his writings or those of other teachers as Holy Writ. How many disturbances, how many executioners of conscience rose up for us because we said that it was not God but Augustine who said some things in his book *de poenitentia*, as that we should repent wholly and confess purely to our own priest. Even if Augustine had said these things, by what authority do they oppress consciences for which Christ died? But now, Augustine indeed did not write that book, but it is spurious. You see, in ch. 15

of it, the author cites Augustine himself. Nevertheless, on the basis of these lies, that man of sin, the pope, along with his canonists and scholastics does not create for us articles of faith when he shamelessly cites Augustine in his decretal letters concerning repentance, dist. 1:"May he who is sorry for his sin be considered, God-willing."

When we speak about repentance on the basis of Scripture, we do not understand actively some contrition, that is, that they imagine sorrow which they assume voluntarily or at least (as they call it) some attrition, that is, some slight displeasure with sin by which they are not beaten to the ground [or contrite]. They rather want to beat themselves into the ground and imagine something which we do not understand as some human satisfaction before God. In this way, we prepare poorly the way of the Lord with John, who cries out:"Prepare the way of the Lord to receive the grace of Christ, our Savior." If we were to teach that we receive forgiveness through our active or passive contritions and by our works or confessions or satisfactions, why do you condemn us with those voluntary and self-chosen religious scruples which you have invented contrary to the Christian faith (Col. 2)?

Rather, when we speak about repentance or contrition as we call it, we ourselves understand a true embarrassment within ourselves and true terrors of the judgment of God and death and pains of conscience over sin. Because the light and Word of the Lord, as they go ahead before Christ, that is, because the preaching of repentance inflames and illumines with its flashing so that not only do those crass wickednesses fall, but even the hidden ones such as are ignorance of God, neglectful contempt of God, our own cupidity, the pursuit of glory and wealth, negligence, and trust in ourselves; I say, because of all this, we see the impurity not only of our own works, but also of our nature and what terrible evils and damnation are ours from that sin which we contracted from our first parents and which we call"original sin."

This contrition is not a voluntarily-assumed sorrow for sins, as they say. Rather, repentance is a gift from God, for the person to whom God does not give it does not have the true repentance of which we are now speaking. Furthermore, God gives repentance through the preaching of repentance or through the preaching of the Law, which the Gospel uses to prepare the way for Christ. Rom. 1: "The wrath of God is revealed, etc." Scripture speaks in this way, 2 Tim. 2: "…if God perhaps give them repentance to acknowledge the truth that those whom the devil has taken prisoner at his will may recover from his snares." Also, Acts 5: "God has exalted this Prince and Savior with His right hand to grant Israel repentance and the remission of sins"; and ch. 11: "Had God therefore given repentance to life to the Gentiles?"

However, you are asking how much sorrow and terror there are in repentance or contrition. I respond. Inasmuch as the repentance about which we speak is the gift of God, we cannot prescribe to God the manner in which He terrifies me through the sin which the Law reveals. The scholastic doctors cite that passage of Jer. 6 which speaks of the Babylonian Captivity: "Mourn as for an only-begotten son with bitter weeping, because the destroyer will come upon you suddenly." That they not bring down others or even themselves if they were not to sense the greatest sorrows, they have been compelled to feign that imperfect contrition which they call "attrition." We interpret this as an imperfect displeasure about the sins we have committed.

Furthermore, we see that some people also come with joy to Christ, as Matthew, Zacchaeus, and others. We also read about the Gentiles, Acts 13: "When the Gentiles heard, they rejoiced and glorified the Word of the Lord, and as many as believed were foreordained for eternal life." However, this very joy testified that they were experiencing sorrow and terrors of conscience because of their sin. After all, people do not take up the Gospel and Christ in the

Gospel except those who know that they and their entire lot have been condemned. They would wish to have God kindly-disposed to them, if that were possible, as Christ says: "The poor have the Gospel preached to them." Indeed, we know what happens, even to the saints, when they are abandoned in temptation and in the horror of the judgments of God and of death, namely, that they are forced to cry out: "Lord, in Your anger do not, etc."

In the meantime, I have been speaking about the definition and subject of repentance about which we read: "Repent!" In our schools and before the congregation it has now been accepted that penitence be taken for the whole turning [or conversion] to God. For the sake of teaching, we say that repentance is not only contrition but that it also has two parts, namely, contrition and faith, which the one word "repentance" includes, although we say it with two words. "Repent, for the kingdom of heaven has come near."

In the last chapter of Luke, Christ speaks of repentance and the remission of sins. The one is the preaching of the Law; the other, the preaching of the Gospel or of faith, as we have said before. These are as different as hell and heaven unless mortification and having new life not differ. Why, then, do we teach in this way?

I respond. We are not contending nor prescribing that each person teach in this way, provided he not teach contrary to the truth of the Gospel. If you speak in the customary manner of Scripture, separate these two—repentance and faith—but know that repentance is empty which faith does not follow, as was the repentance of Esau, Saul, Judas, etc. That which the Papists teach is false and nothing other than blasphemy. As they now use it, the Papists take repentance for the conversion of the sinner by which a person who is the son of perdition becomes a son of salvation and is saved from his sins. In this repentance, they teach nothing about faith.

Against this wickedness, we take this word "repentance" in the accepted manner and say that it has two parts that we not teach (like an Antichrist) the remission of sins without faith in Christ, as we said earlier about the three parts of sophist repentance. You see, God gives us that salutary repentance about which Scripture speaks to encourage us to faith in the promised grace, just as, according to Paul, the Law is our schoolmaster for Christ, and in this way the Law becomes salutary, although it nevertheless does not have salvation but is the minister of death.

You have read this before: "God gave the Gentiles repentance to life"; and in Acts 5: "God has exalted Him as Priest and Savior with His right hand to give repentance and remission of sins to Israel." In Mark 1, we read: "John baptized and preached the Baptism of repentance for the remission of sins." That is, he preached that Christ was coming and baptized with the Baptism of repentance, as Paul says (Acts 19), in the coming Christ through whom those who believe the preaching and Baptism of John have the remission of sins. For he speaks in this way about Christ: "Behold the Lamb of God who takes away the sins of the world."

Here Matthew is explaining the Baptism of repentance in this way: "He was baptizing them in the Jordan as they confessed their sins." And John the Baptist said: "I baptize you with water for your repentance," that is, that you may acknowledge your errors and sins and take up your Savior whom the Law and the Prophets promised. These things we say in passing about the form of our words. We shall go into detail when we teach against the ungodly teaching of those who teach the remission of sins without faith in Christ.

We are not speaking outside of Scripture when we say that salutary repentance has two parts—contrition and faith—because Scripture is in the habit of speaking in this way, as in Mark 1: "... preaching the Baptism of repentance for the forgiveness of sins."

Let us therefore return to those things which we began to discuss. John says: "Repent. The kingdom of heaven is at hand." The Gospel or the New Testament preserves for itself this office of preaching of the Law or of repentance, as we have said, so that the whole world may become answerable to God, Rom. 3 and John 16: "The Holy Spirit will reprove the world of sin, of judgment and of righteousness." Both sinners and saints are thrown down by this thunderbolt, for neither has permission to be upright before God. Rather, they are terrified and despairing. This is how true repentance begins.

Here a person hears this judgment: "All people are nothing. You must become other people and act in a different way." Here no one is just. This is not active contrition nor fictitious repentance, but passive contrition, true repentance, true sorrow of heart, anguish, and death.

However, when the Law or the preaching of repentance performs its duty only and alone without the addition of the Gospel, then repentance is useless, death, hell, and despair, as in the cases of Saul and Judas. Paul says: "The Law kills through sin"; and again: "The Law works wrath, etc." Therefore, the new testament immediately adds to this office of preaching repentance the comforting promise of grace through the Gospel, which people must believe.

John says: "The kingdom of heaven is at hand. Believe the Gospel. Receive the forgiveness of sins in Christ." Here only faith in Christ justifies, and "there is no other name given under heaven to people in which we must be saved." "There is salvation in no one else." This salvation, comfort, and remission of sins which the Gospel offers us in different ways, namely, through the Word, through the Sacraments, through the power of the keys, through mutual conversation, because, according to the Law (Mat. 28), and as we also sing in the psalm, "Manifold and abundant is redemption in the presence of God."

This repentance endures in Christians throughout their lives because they wrestle with the remnant of sin in the flesh so long as they live (Rom. 7), indeed, not through their own powers but through the gift of the Holy Spirit, which gift follows the remission of sins. We read in Rom. 8: "If by the Holy Spirit you mortify the flesh, you will live." This gift purges and sweeps away daily and endlessly the remnant of sin in the flesh and tries to create a truly purged person. The pope, those skilled in the Law, theologians, scholastics—all people—do not know this, for this is a teaching which has been revealed to people from heaven, and among the wicked little saints we call it "heresy" and "the doctrines of demons."

The kingdom of heaven is called "the kingdom of God" or "the kingdom of Christ" as opposed to the head of the serpent, the kingdom of the devil, the kingdom of death, the kingdom of sin and therefore is contrary to the kingdom and tyranny of the Law and against the wrath of God, under which are all people. For death ruled through sin from Adam all the way to Moses. However, through Moses (that is, through the revealed Law) sin killed more seriously and caused despair, until the Gospel should come which promises remission of sins and eternal life for the sake of Christ.

This is the blessing of all nations in the seed of Abraham, for all who were cursed and condemned are blessed by the Gospel of Christ. This truly is the kingdom of heaven, where God now rules in Christ and where He gives eternal righteousness not because of our merits but only by the goodness of God who loves us and gave up His only-begotten Son for us while we were still His enemies and wicked. He also sealed us with His Holy Spirit, namely with the faith which He gave us through the Gospel of promise that we may believe this and, believing, become the children and heirs of God. Here we become the kingdom of God and kings and priests in Christ. Here the head of the serpent is crushed according to the promise made to Adam through the Seed of the woman, Christ. Here the sentence of damnation and terror gives way, something which could have happened through no powers, no works, no righteousness of the Law. Here we recognize God, namely, that He is our Father in Christ, and that terrible blindness, contempt, unbelief, unrighteousness, etc. contracted through original sin perish. Christ speaks in this way: "The Law and the Prophets were until John; and from that time the kingdom of God has been preached as Gospel." Paul said to the Galatians: "...until the Seed which was promised should come."

Here, however, you should not look only at that time before Christ was revealed on earth, but also at this time in individual people endlessly through all the world when people had not yet received Christ through the Gospel. For there sin and death ruled, and there was no remedy until that Seed of eternal blessedness came through the Gospel. You see, those who feel seriously the tyranny of the Law which reveals sin and the wrath of God from heaven would perish forever, as did Saul and Judas, unless that consolation and preaching of the Gospel of the kingdom of God follow immediately. "So long as people do not believe in the Son of God, the wrath of God remains upon them all," John the Baptist says. But where they receive the Son of God with faith, there there can be no wrath of God, for the Father is pleased in Him.

God respects nothing beside this Son. He who believes in Him is a child of God and heir of the kingdom. It is only by His mercy and not by any merit of ours that He takes us up. Here a person may not boast about his own wisdom or righteousness, for "no one knows the things which have been hidden in God from eternity" (Rom. 16). "No one knows the Father except the Son and him to whom the Son wanted to reveal the Father" (Mat. 11). Paul says that no righteousness is approved before God except that "which is through faith in Christ" (Phi. 3). "Let the wise be silent here then, for those who say they are wise have become fools" (Rom. 1). "Let also the upright be silent, that is, righteous, who hear this. Harlots and publicans will go into the kingdom of heaven ahead of you" (Mat. 21).

If human wisdom and righteousness cannot boast here but ought to give glory to God and confess that they are nothing, it would be great madness and the greatest contempt for God not to condemn the known foolishness and the unrighteousness of which people are aware on the basis of the Second Table of Moses. This is something we said against those impenitent people who learn to sin from the preaching of grace, when they hear that they are not the righteous but harlots and publicans or sinners who are saved, and who don't want to hear that sinners are called to repentance that they might accept Christ, as Christ says: "I have not come to call the righteous but sinners to repentance."

Also, against those who know that human wisdom is ignorant of God and of the righteousness of God, they very foolishly neglect the true wisdom of God and do not learn how to discern between the Law and the Gospel and between civic and Christian righteousness. As a result, it happens that in temptations and when they suffer the attacks of sectarians and false doctrine, they know no more of the Gospel than do a horse and mule.

Add as a comfort to the heathen that here Jewish blood must also keep silent. It is nothing that Jews, born of holy fathers, bear in their flesh the circumcision covenant of God, unless they receive this kingdom of heaven to which that election of that people and that circumcision used to look according to the promise God made to Abraham: "In your seed, etc." Against these John is immediately preaching here, when he says that the kingdom of heaven is at hand, for they were dreaming about an earthly kingdom for themselves through the Messiah, as the dregs of the Jews still do today, uncertain as they are of the kingdom of heaven. Also later: "Don't say: 'We have Abraham as our father, etc.'" Also, Christ says: "They will come from the east and the west, and they will sit down with Abraham, Isaac, and Jacob in the kingdom of heaven; but the children of the kingdom will be thrown out into outer darkness, where there will be weeping and gnashing of teeth."

Because all these human things are nothing and condemned, and because the preaching of repentance and the kingdom of heaven are promised and are the preaching of the Gospel and of grace, John the Evangelist expressed that in this way: "They have not been born of blood nor of the will of the flesh nor of the will of man but of God." As I have said, therefore it is mercy alone and not our merit that "we are taken up in Christ out of the kingdom of darkness into the kingdom of heaven" (Col. 1, etc.). This is something which John clearly adds here when he says about the kingdom of heaven: "It is at hand." For we have approached not by our own powers, merits, or righteousnesses, and we have not deserved it, because we were caught up under the kingdom of death and darkness, so that we don't know whether it existed or what it was. That's how far anyone is from being able to desire the kingdom of heaven. Rather, it has come to us and seeks us out. It has been revealed to us through the Gospel of the only-begotten Son of God and given to us, so that you can understand that there is nothing else than the grace of God in this word.

"...in the wilderness" which lies to the south of Judea.

"...a voice crying..." Although the voice is in the wilderness according to the prophecy, nevertheless it is the voice of the shouting preacher or the voice shouting, so that it rouses all Judea. So do not think that he preached in a corner, which is what the sectarians do first that they may next take over the public cathedrals. You see, God predestined John for this duty of forerunner, as Isaiah and Malachi had foretold, and the boy hid in the wilderness until the time of his calling (about which see Luke 3). However, because God chose this "voice," John, and called him for this, we are sure that God commanded him to baptize, for with this shouting of his or his preaching he was confirming it for believers, just as in John 1 he himself responds from Isaiah to the unworthy priests and Levites that he did baptize. He says: "I am the voice crying in the, etc.," as if to say: "I am preaching the Baptism of repentance not without the calling of God." Therefore, he also says, John 1: "He sent me to baptize, etc." In Luke 7, Christ calls the preaching and Baptism of John "the counsel of God," something which now was so well-known in Judea that the scribes and Pharisees did not dare to mutter when the Lord asked: "Was the Baptism of John of men or of God?"

It is an error but still pleasant and without peril of doctrine that we distinguish in words but not in the actual subject matter between the Baptism of John and that of Christ. But now, when all things are filled with sects and a calumniator could abuse these customary words of Christian teachers, our Philip [Melanchthon] advises in a very holy way that we must not distinguish between the Baptism of John and that of Christ unless we should wish to distinguish persons, namely, between John and Christ, between the servant and his master, between the minister of justification and the actual Justifier, as John says later: "I baptize you with water, but He, etc.," something which no one is asking in this question.

However, we must discern between the Baptism of John and that of the apostles. Both Baptisms are *of* Christ or *in* Christ. But just as John preaches that Christ is going to come, so he baptizes into the coming Christ, just as he clearly says here: "The One who is coming after me…" As the apostles preached Christ who came, so they baptized into the Christ who came. Of what sort the preaching of John and of the apostles is, of such a kind is also their Baptism. The former had a command from God to preach and baptize in Judea, as we have said, that the people there might believe in the coming Christ. But the latter had their command to preach in all the world that people might believe in Christ who had come and who had received power in heaven and on earth to be the Savior of all, both Jews and Gentiles.

After Christ came for His sacrifice and salvation, therefore, it would have been wicked to preach that He had not yet come but was going to come, which is the blasphemy of the Jews today. After all, what would this preaching and Baptism be other than to deny the Christ who had come? As the preaching of John ceased, so also did his very sacred Baptism into the coming Christ cease, after Christ became the ruler, as Daniel had foretold and said: "… until Christ, the Ruler…"

John was going to be the forerunner of the Savior and not another savior, as the angel had told his father: "He himself will go before Him, etc." His father sang: "He will go before the face of the Lord to prepare His ways." Also, there is no one who does not see that this was repeated from Isaiah. You read these things from the mouth of Paul in Acts 19, where we read the following: "John baptized with the Baptism of repentance and said that they should believe in Him who was going to come after him, that is, in Jesus, who is Himself the Christ."

What John the Baptist says later: "Christ will baptize you with the Holy Spirit and with fire," he does not say about the ministry of the Church nor about the Baptism instituted for, and commanded to, the apostles and the Church, and which the Church is preserving, which is "the washing of water in the Word" (Eph. 5). Rather, he says that which the words have about that very thing which the Spirit Himself was obviously going to do through Himself before their eyes and to those very people to whom John preached. For he is prophesying about the obvious giving of the Holy Spirit, who came in fire, as you read in the Acts of the Apostles.

Just as we have it, the apostle before also had faith through the Holy Spirit just as Christ responded to Peter when he confessed: "You are the Christ, the Son of the living God": "Blessed are you, Simon, son of Jonah. Flesh and blood have not revealed this to you but My Father, who is in heaven," namely, by the Holy Spirit.

Moreover, that you may understand this, Christ Himself says, Acts 1: "John baptized with water, but not many days from now you will receive the Baptism with the Holy Spirit." In Acts 11,

Peter speaks about the account of Cornelius: "When I had begun to speak to the Gentiles, the Holy Spirit fell upon them just as He fell on us in the beginning. Furthermore, I recalled the word of the Lord, just as He had spoken.'"John indeed baptized with water, but you will be baptized with the Holy Spirit,'" something even Peter himself had said on the day of Pentecost had been foretold through Joel, as you read in Acts 2.

You see, then, that John had not been saying these things about the Baptism of Christ which Christ instituted for His Church, although the Holy Spirit is also given in it, but in secret, as the account of Acts 10 has it in the account of Cornelius, after this Baptism with which Christ Himself baptized the household of Cornelius with the Holy Spirit and with fire without Peter. In fact, Peter was not even thinking of this, much less hoping for it. Peter commanded our Baptism with water which Christ instituted to be added to the same people whom Christ had baptized from heaven with the Holy Spirit and with fire, for people cannot hold in contempt what Christ has instituted, when the Holy Spirit is present, the way some people hold the Sacraments of Christ in contempt today because of the spirit of the devil, and these are people who boast of their wisdom and spirit.

Some sectarian who otherwise despises the institution of Christ in the Sacraments had said this without hesitation: "What's the need of baptizing with water those whom Christ Himself baptized with the Holy Spirit and with fire?" But let us allow them to say that. You read this: "While Peter was still speaking, the Holy Spirit fell upon all who were listening to the Word, and they began to speak in tongues, etc. Then Peter responded: 'Can anyone forbid water so that those who received the Holy Spirit just as we did may not be baptized?' And he commanded them to be baptized in the name of Christ." Here you hear that this was a Baptism with water, just as John says about his Baptism: "I baptize you with water."

In the meantime, we have to say these things because of the actual truthfulness of the Word of God and of history, because there once were and still now are said to be some in India who are called "Jacobites," if I remember correctly,[12] and if it is true that people say that they were feeling from these words of John about Christ that we must not only use water for Baptism but also fire and that infants must receive some mark or other through fire. Certainly Origen wrote about some female disciple of his who was a catechumen and who was crowned with martyrdom that she had received the baptism of fire, as you read in Eusebius, *hist. eccles.*, Bk. 6, ch. 4. It appears that her executioners prevented her from receiving Baptism with water.

If, however, they feel that we must apply external fire to burn, why do they not also apply the Holy Spirit externally to the Baptism of water? After all, he does not only say: "He will baptize you with fire," but: "He will baptize you with fire and with the Holy Spirit." Or why don't they submerge the whole person into fire when they hear here that the Baptism of fire is not some mark made by fire or branding? However, we believe that they are not so stupid as to wish to attempt such Baptism. That's what happens to those who abandon the institution and command of Christ and snatch up another word which has not been commanded them.

John says about Christ: "He will baptize with fire and the Holy Spirit." Those people snatch this up without a mandate, as if they themselves be Christ and more than John and the apostles. The institution of the Baptism of water says: "Go and teach all nations, baptizing them in the name of the Father and of the Son and of the Holy Spirit." This is the Baptism of water with which Christ was baptized in the Jordan, and the way the eunuch baptized Queen Candace in the river, about which Paul says that Christ washed His bride with the washing of water in the Word. Those who want to

12    One possible source of Bugenhagen's account of the Jacobite Church is *The Travels* of Marco Polo, Book III, chapter xxxv.

create a better Baptism when they add fire (which Christ did not institute) hold this institution in contempt.

There are those who say that Christ is now baptizing with water and the holy Spirit, but in secret, as is true according to those words of Christ: "Unless a person have been born again of water and the Holy Spirit, etc." They also say that on the last day He is going to baptize His elect with fire when, purged by fire of death and every corruption, they will receive deliverance through Jesus Christ, our Lord. Although they may say this, provided they take nothing away from the grace of Christ which alone purges us; nevertheless, nothing of this has to do with the institution of Baptism, and nothing of this has to do with these words of John.

Also, who would rebuke either the ancient teachers or us who teach in a godly way that we are born again of water and the Holy Spirit, who is fire, so that the conjunction ["and"] is taken expositively: "We are baptized with the Holy Spirit, who is fire," if we are permitted to explain this as a known through a more unknown and the matter itself through an allegory of itself, leaving all the other words in their proper meaning and making the rest an allegory from fire alone?

No one is saying that this is a bad explanation if I shall have said that He who is the Holy Spirit in Himself is fire as a result of His effect. After all, with the preaching of the Gospel the Holy Spirit first burns, embarrasses, condemns, and causes to perish all our sins, for "He reproves the world of sin, of judgment and of righteousness." Next, He illumines with faith and the understanding of God and His will; He sets on fire with the love of God, invocation, and a godly life so that the many waters of tribulation cannot extinguish this holy flame and fire of the Holy Spirit. Although we may say these things in truth, and although it most certainly is true that even now in the Church, Christ baptizes with the Holy Spirit; nevertheless, we must confirm them on the basis of other passages of Scripture, for here John does not say such things.

Similarly, we say not badly that Christ baptizes with the Holy Spirit, something which no one denies about the Baptism which He instituted, and with fire, namely, the fire of tribulation, just as Scripture often uses that allegory of fire in 1 Peter 1 and elsewhere, namely, that that fire proves and purges us as fire does to gold. Otherwise, "some believe for a time and in time of temptation go away." But what do these things have to do with the Sacrament of Baptism where there is no respect for tribulations or sufferings in human work, but only in Christ as the Cleanser and Savior? This is not that I am saying that in the sure words of Christ's institution nothing is left certain if we were permitted everywhere to corrupt the truthfulness of history with uncertain allegories. You see, when Scripture uses the allegory of fire for tribulation, it explains itself there so that no one doubts that it is taken in this way, something which does not happen here. But what's the need for these things here? The words of John the Baptist here do not intend this.

It is plausible, however, that some think that John is saying this here: "Christ will baptize you Jews—some, those who have believed, with the Holy Spirit for life, and some, who have not believed, with the inextinguishable fire." This opinion seems to agree with what follows: "And He will sweep carefully His threshing floor and will gather the wheat into His granary, but the chaff He will burn in the inextinguishable fire." However, as I am unable to accept Baptism as damnation and destruction, so also I should not. John surely is not speaking about such a Baptism.

I have been presenting to you, my beloved hearers, these various interpretations where John says: "He will baptize, etc.," not that you test those who are in the habit of interpreting Scripture in different ways and tear it into a thousand shapes, but rather, that you be wary of them. They boast of great wisdom and spirit as if someone else cannot even imagine anything in a passage of Scripture (if this is interpreting Scripture and not rather making it unclear). We are certain that there are such unlearned people who are ignorant of Scripture, because they do not see that one certain way of thinking of the Holy Spirit. Otherwise, who would dare to assert in the same passage of Scripture another and often diverse way of thinking? It also happens that they often do not speak such good opinions (although those must be proved elsewhere) such as I have presented to you, and such very holy ones as the blessed Augustine has spoken, although not on this passage. Rather, it happens that they speak absurd opinions which are foreign to Scripture. This is the habit of the pope, as when he interprets the word of Christ against Christ: "You are Peter, etc."

Therefore, you have here from me an excellent example of a different interpretation for being careful, for although there are some things which I have said which are true in themselves or which we can confirm from other passages of Scripture (or at least which have nothing dangerous to the faith in the case of the godly); nevertheless, all these interpretations of which we must be wary are false interpretations of this passage everywhere except one, and we must seek out that one which is true, using faith as our schoolmistress, just as Paul says that interpretation or teaching must be analogous to faith.

Nevertheless, I do not see anything which is not dangerous when, in the meantime, one denies the truthfulness of history because of a false interpretation; and thus it nearly happens that an opportunity for error is provided to disquieted spirits, as happens to those who out of this passage create for themselves a Baptism of fire.

Our own waverings and thanklessness toward God, our distaste and contempt for the Word, our presumption of wisdom and our neglect have led us away from Scripture, something which you see even in this one passage. Few people even until today have seen this interpretation of Scripture which we have shown to be true from what happened afterward and from the word of Christ and of Peter.

"…confessing their sins." That is, they came confessing that they were sinners, acknowledging their sins and condemning them. In this way, they confessed that they were repentant and believed the preaching of John. He certainly is crazy who thinks that Matthew is saying something here about auricular confession. Here, therefore, I shall speak not even a word about this but perhaps I shall speak about it elsewhere in a more appropriate place.

"And when he saw…" He adds this necessarily in his account because the prophets and preachers preached by the command of God repentance to all people that they should recover from their errors and sins so that the whole world became guilty before God, as we read in Rom. 3. Those petty, little saints, however, and those who in their own judgment were righteous, such as here were the Pharisees and Sadducees, held them in contempt and judged that this preaching of repentance had nothing to do with them. They thought that the preaching was not bad but did not pertain to them because they were righteous, but rather had to do with sinners, that is, with publicans and whores. In Luke 15, Christ calls those "righteous" who were in no need of repentance, as they themselves felt, "vainly puffed up as they were in the mind of their flesh and blinded by human teachings," as Paul says (Col. 2).

The Holy Spirit, therefore, who through the preaching of the Word reproves the whole world and condemns all our sins quite strongly and harshly reproves this class of petty, little saints who are unwilling to be sinners and have been condemned because of sin, or if they do see their sin, see it only as a sin against the Second Table (for they do not at all understand the First). These people nevertheless trust in their own works, righteousnesses, invented worship, and satisfactions and, briefly, as we read in Luke 18, trust in themselves as righteous, and despise the rest, etc.

John therefore calls them "a generation of vipers," not only because they come from a bad beginning, being conceived and born in sin (that is, the bad beginning of all people), but much more because beyond that natural blindness of their corrupt nature they also had wicked fathers, that is, teachers of human doctrines, of invented worship and of the false righteousness of works, which is true idolatry and ignorance of the First Commandment by which the wicked person says in his heart: "There is no God."

How does it happen, then, that prostitutes and publicans acknowledge their sins more quickly and become converted to God than those wise little "saintlets" who despise both God and people and who are not as righteous as they appear but liars, of unsound doctrine and savage murder, hating those who profess the Word, as Christ depicts them in His own colors ( John 8)? They are "blind leaders of the blind" (Mat. 15). They themselves have become infected with the doctrines of demons and the true venom of the devil and generate disciples infected with the same venom. They themselves perish from the heat of generating, and they produce children or disciples who have to perish in the same way later, just as we read about the intercourse and birth of snakes.

However, John goes on and says: "Who has warned you, etc.?" He is signifying that there is no class of humans more blinded against the truthfulness of God than this. It is as if he is saying: "I am not surprised about others who acknowledge their sins, come to their senses and give glory to the Word of God. However, I am surprised by you who can be persuaded to come to your senses and not suffer the coming wrath of God." Moreover, he says "the *coming* wrath" which was going to come now according to the predictions of the prophets for the faithless Jews to be cast down in body and spirit for also having lost the kingdom of the Messiah or Christ and the priesthood. John speaks about this wrath of God later in great detail. We also read in John 3: "The wrath of God remains upon him who does not believe in the Son of God." All these things are true about hypocrites and the pseudo-righteous of all times.

"Bring forth fruits therefore..." After chiding them, he admonishes and threatens. He admonishes that those who already want to appear repentant and believers of the preaching truly repent from their heart and come to their senses. He also threatens that those are going to perish unless they do come to their senses, that God will not regard them as the children of Abraham, that the ax has been set to the root of the tree and that the chaff will be burned in the unquenchable fire. Today those among us who kept boasting that they were spiritual are found through the preaching of the Gospel to be the kingdom of the Antichrist, and I perhaps shall speak about these in the following chapter regarding the third temptation of Christ. You see how those perish who because of their wickedness are the manifest enemies of Christ (about which see Psa. 2).

The pseudo-righteous (namely the common monks and others) try to confirm from these words: "Produce fruits worthy of repentance," their own mandates, satisfactions for sins, and all those human righteousnesses and invented religions and ungodly sacrifices from human traditions, although nevertheless John says not a word here that we must make satisfaction for our sins through such satisfactions. In fact, he speaks here in a far different manner, namely: "The kingdom of heaven is at hand."

Clearly, with that wicked opinion of satisfactions they are denying the Gospel and the blood of Christ and the mercy of the Father. From these, we do not *earn* remission (which would not be "remission"). Rather, the remission of sins is gracious. The sincere Gospel of Christ declares that remission is not due to any merits or works of ours, nor is it owed on the basis of the Law of God. In this way, I am saying that on the basis of the divine Law those things cannot truly exist which become the surety of making satisfaction

for sins, for this is idolatry against the greatest and first commandment, without which all the other commandments are nothing before God, for it teaches to trust only in the kindness of the Father,
etc. Read this in the *Apology of the Augsburg Confession*.

Therefore, it is ridiculous or childish to interpret these
words: "Produce fruits worthy of repentance," in this way: "Produce
enough on behalf of your sins either in the world or in the monas-
tery." When did John preach this? He cries out: "The Lamb of God
takes away the sins of the world," so that the divine remission of sins
is not human satisfaction for sins.

What, then, is the native sense of these words? I respond.
They want what they sound like: "Make fruit," as is customary in
Scripture, is to produce or bear fruit, just as plants and trees do. After all, this metaphor comes from those, as Psa. 1: "All the things that
he does will prosper," something which we know very well also from
this passage. For John adds immediately: "Every tree which does not
produce good fruit, etc." Furthermore, we recognize whether a tree
is good or bad from its fruit, as Christ also says (Mat. 7). There He
explains the metaphor clearly and says: "You will know them from
their fruits." That is, you will recognize them from the fruits which
they make or produce. However, He does not say: "Through their
fruits they will make satisfaction for their sins," because He says they
are rather wicked rascals and hypocrites who preach the doctrines
of demons, which is not to mention that Christ does not acknowledge satisfactory sinners much less approve them with His Word.

Here we have to indicate these things so grossly because of
the very gross ignorance of these "grammarians" by which we have
taught their wickedness so far from these words.

These words "Produce fruits worthy of repentance" or "Produce fruits which befit repentance" want this: "You Pharisees and
Sadducees have come here for the Baptism of repentance. However,
if after it you truly want to be good trees (that is, truly repentant

to the depths of our heart and believing in the preaching of God), make (that is, produce in your conscience before God according to the First Table of the Law and outwardly before the world according to the Second Table of the Law) fruits worthy of repentance. That is, abandon your errors, do not teach human doctrines, don't mislead others, behave well according to the Word of God, serve others according to your calling." This is what we say commonly and truthfully: "Repentance is the new life on the basis of the Word of God, and Baptism is our mortification, that afterward we may live to God. But if you do not abandon your blasphemies, false worship, misleading, plundering, hypocrisy, contempt for the Word of God, and other sins, but afterwards love and defend them; from these fruits it will become apparent to you before God and to others before the world that you are still bad trees, that you are not truly repentant but are adding greater sins yet to your prior ones, and that you have already tried to deceive even God with the truth which has already been revealed. In this case, you must perish along with other hypocrites by the judgment of God."

With those words, John was signifying that he saw in spirit some Pharisees and Sadducees coming with a pretending heart to Baptism and pretending upstanding character because of the common crowd, in just the same way as Simon Magus came to the preaching and Baptism of the apostles and as the betrayer Judas kept appearing to be a true Christian. Saul, a holy king, namely, whom God had chosen for the kingdom as He called Judas to his apostleship, and some Evangelicals today whom we must admonish and frighten with these words of John that they truly come to their senses, love the Gospel, believe in Christ, and confess both the teaching and life according to the Word of God; —I say, if these still feel their sins in this body of sin, nevertheless, let them not fall away from that confidence in the mercy of God and in the remission of sins in Christ. These are the worthy fruits of Christian repentance.

However, if they approve of the ancient errors and abominations of the Papists and despise others, etc.; what business do they have with the Gospel and Sacraments of Christ? They are still in their sins. For there is true remission of sins in Christ, as we read in the psalm: "Blessed are those whose iniquities are forgiven, etc." There however we have the addition: "...and in whose spirit there is no guile."

See what I am saying from Luke 3. When John requires fruits worthy of repentance (that is, a new life), he is not changing civil and political ordinances, summoning people to abandon their public calling and duties and live with him in the wilderness, there to live and torture themselves in this way, doing this and that to take away their sins and to increase their merits. He is not inviting them to keep these and those monastic rules and thus clothe themselves, etc. All this is Antichristian justification. Rather, he is admonishing those who have already become believers and who have been justified by faith to have love for their neighbors that those who have an overflow may support the rest. He says: "Let him who has two coats, etc." Publicans should demand nothing from people beyond what the legal taxes are. Soldiers should not be harmful but content with their wages. That is, each person should serve faithfully in his own calling as if he is serving the Lord Christ. Peter and Paul strongly admonish this to servants and subjects as well as to masters and magistrates.

Notice that Luke says that John spoke these words to the crowds: "You generation of vipers, etc." However, when he makes no mention of the Pharisees and Sadducees, we understand from Matthew that he said this principally to the Pharisees and Sadducees who were in that crowd, for Christ also often preached against them separately. Nevertheless, those words pertain correctly to the whole crowd which permitted the Pharisees and Sadducees to mislead it, according to those words: "If a blind person leads a blind person, both fall into the pit." This is just as the Holy Spirit in Paul (1 Tim. 4) not only calls the teachers "erring spirits and devils" but also their students alone who are condemned of error and says: "They will defect from the faith and cling to the spirits of error and doctrines of demons, etc."

"Do not be of this mind, etc."; that is: "Don't have confidence in the fact that you were born of the flesh of Abraham and the patriarchs because God promised that to Abraham and his seed. You must also remember how you were warned even in Moses and the prophets about the unbelieving Jews. Therefore, it is necessary for you to know that the believing children of Abraham are those who are going to be blessed and who believe through the Seed of Abraham which is Christ, as it is written: 'The children of Abraham are those who believe as Abraham did and who because of their faith act as did Abraham, as they obey the Word of God,' just as Christ (John 9) and Paul (Gal. 3) declare. 'You are all the children of God because you have believed in Christ Jesus, for all who have been baptized have put on Christ. There is neither Jew nor Greek; neither slave nor free, neither male nor female, for you are all one in Jesus Christ. If however you belong to Christ, you therefore are the seed of Abraham, and heirs according to the promise. Those who are of the faith therefore are blessed along with faithful Abraham, for as many as are of the works of the Law are subject to the curse, etc.'"

The Jews were being very presumptuous as if they were holy from the nobility or saintliness of their lineage, for they were the people of God who could not perish. But they were unwilling to see that God requires faith. They forgot all the curses of the Law and the threats against the unbelieving Jews, contrary to what the Evangelist John says: "His own did not accept Him, but as many as did accept Him, those He gave the power to become the children of God, who believe on His name, who are not of the blood, etc."

The believing repentant or those who come to their senses say, Isa. 63: "You, O Lord, are our Father. Abraham does not know us. Israel is ignorant of us, but You are our Father, our Redeemer, and Your name is from everlasting." Here John warns them and says: "God is strong enough to raise up from these stones the children of Abraham," that is, those who are going to believe as Abraham did, "but if you have not believed the way as Abraham did, something which was reckoned to them for righteousness, you have been cast away."

Surely the stones to which John pointed in the wilderness were not of the seed of Abraham, nor did they have the Law of Moses. They did not worship God nor have either divine or human traditions. They were deaf, dumb, and blind, without heart, without life. In this way, John is pointing to the Gentiles, who were foreign to the state of Israel, as also Paul says in Eph. 2. In this way, he preaches the true and pure grace of God, just as I have said about the conversion of the Gentiles earlier on ch. 2. Paul speaks to the Romans about these on the basis of Hosea: "I shall call those who are not My people 'My people; etc.'"; and from Isaiah: "Those who were not looking for Me have found Me, etc."

"Already the ax, etc." That it—what has been foretold to you—is about to take place. Both God and people will cast away the unbelieving Jews, and only their remnant will be saved, something which Paul again cites from Isaiah: "Even if the number of the children of Israel have been as the sand of the sea, a remnant will be saved."

Matthew calls the judgment of God an "ax," which was now threatening those who despised Christ or His Gospel. He goes on with the same simile and says: "Every tree, etc." After he condemned the trust of that type in this way, he now also condemns appropriately their trust in their works and righteousness. Those Pharisees and Sadducees show nothing less than that they are not producing good fruit when they do many things according to their human traditions, serving (as they think) God. For this reason, they dare to say:"I am not like other people, etc." Consequently, the Pharisees (that is, the "separated") behave as do the Sadducees (that is, the "justified").

All the things that they do, they do either on the basis of human traditions or for appearance's sake from the Law of God (which requires a heart, that is, that you do what you are commanded on the basis of the Law); I say, all these things they do that people may see them (Mat. 6) and that they may have merit before God, and that they may be righteous as a result of their own works, just as the Pharisee says: "I thank you, God, that I am not like other people, etc." We shall speak about these in Mat. 7, where Christ even excludes from His Kingdom those who preached the Gospel, cast out evil spirits, and performed miracles in the name of Christ, because they wanted Him to take them up to heaven because of their confidence in their works and not only because of Christ alone. You see, they were making out of divine works done in the name of Christ very wicked works for themselves, that is, idolatry.

But if Christ is asserting this about such people, what hope do you have with regard to others? The Evangelist John also spoke in this way:"…not of the will of the flesh nor of the will of man, etc." Paul cites Moses:"[It is] not of the will nor of the running but of God having mercy."

From that false confidence, which is true idolatry, it must happen that these so-called "righteous" and hypocrites who boast about the Law not only do not keep the First Commandment but also dash against it terribly and sin and are blinded against it more than other sinners. John therefore warns them to come to their senses and believe truly, and that each should serve his calling according to the Word of God, which is doing everything from faith, etc.

"I indeed baptize, etc." [The Evangelist] John describes this more expressly (ch. 1). You see, because they considered John [the

Baptist] so great that they could believe that he was the Christ (as we read in Luke 3), how did they keep asking Him, as also in John 1: "Who are you, etc.?" Although he has sanctified in the womb, he was far lower than Christ and admits that he must be compared with Him not even in the least and that he was unworthy even to carry His sandals. That is, he admits that his position is merely to provide a very useful ministry for Him by which he makes clear that Jesus Christ is not only a man but is also God. Otherwise, he is certainly a man worthy of receiving obedience from a person.

You see this confession of John the Baptist about the divinity of Christ even more clearly in John 1 and 2. Here he adds: " He will baptize you with the Holy Spirit and with fire," as if to say: "I in the meantime am performing no miracle," as we also read in John 10. He will declare with portents and miracles that in heaven and on earth He is the Son of God and the salvation of the world as you will see after His resurrection, and He will become for you what Joel foretold, etc. You read this in Acts 2.

"[He who cometh] after me," that is, "After my ministry, after I have finished the business of preaching and forerunning, I have received a mandate from God that He [Christ] Himself will come, namely, to perform His office, and He will begin with the preaching of the Gospel of His kingdom on earth. I then will stop, but this will not be the end of His kingdom." Malachi foretold this about John and Christ: "Behold I shall send My angel, etc." Thus, understand this also in the Gospel of John, for we cannot take this to be a reference to persons because John and Christ were on earth at the same time, nor do we take "John" to mean someone else who is speaking in the Gospel of John in this way: "I baptize you with water, but you don't know the One who stands in your midst." With this word, he confesses Christ as present, but he adds: "It is He who is going to come after me, who is preferred ahead of me; that is, who is more worthy than me and superior to me, and I am not worthy of untying His shoestring." Again: "He must increase, but I must decrease. He who comes from above is over all people, etc." John says that they must not trust in him, a man, regardless of how holy he may appear, but in Jesus Christ, who is both God and man, that is, the Savior and Mediator between God and man, who gives the Holy Spirit and speaks the Word of God. What business do we have with the fathers when they teach against the righteousness of Christ and the sincerity of the Gospel? What do we have to do with the merits and invocation of the saints and the rest of Papist idolatry? Etc.

"...whose fan, etc." He is saying the same thing with a different comparison as he had said before about the ax and trees. The Father has appointed Christ to be the Judge of the living and the dead (Acts 10). He gathers the wheat, that is, the faithful, into His granary, into His Church, into the kingdom of heaven. He considers those His people and makes them the children of God. He will separate the chaff, that is unbelievers and hypocrites, which presses down the wheat, and hand it over for temporal and eternal destruction.

See how carefully John offers his preaching of repentance which, in the meantime, might have remained fruitless (as we said earlier), except that he preached repentance through the Gospel, something which Matthew also describes here, namely, that John did this when he said: "The kingdom of heaven is at hand." You see this much more clearly in John 1 and 3, in the testimonies of John regarding Christ.

Now follows through the Gospel the revelation of Christ to the world and of His kingdom on earth.

"Then Jesus came from Galilee to the Jordan, etc." After the description of the forerunner, John, along with his preaching and Baptism, then Christ came to proclaim Himself to the world, but first to His Jews according to the promises made to the fathers

(Rom. 15), as John had said: "He who will come after me, etc." This Christ, the Son of God, became a man for us to become a sacrifice on the cross for us. He begins His kingdom through the publication of the Gospel on earth, and later He sends it to all nations, saying: "Go into all the world, etc."

The prophets formerly complained because He preached this to the Jews, as we read in Isa. 53: "Who has believed our report and to whom was the arm of the Lord revealed?" You see, today both Gentiles and Jews (that is, all people every day) take offense at the form of the cross.

The carnal Jews therefore await in their dreams another Christ and another kingdom of Christ on earth which nonetheless will be better before God than they are now. They do not understand the promises about the woman's Seed, about Abraham's Seed, and others made about Christ in the Prophets and the Psalms. They do not see their sin and its condemnation, and that they need Christ as their Redeemer. Blinded as they are, they cannot see that this is the greatest glory in the kingdom of Christ: that Christ cleanses His Church through His Holy Spirit with the washing of water in the Word, who forgives all sins, creates children of God, triumphs within us against sin, death, and the devil, and gifts us with eternal life so that through Him we say with confidence: "O death, where now is your victory?" All the kingdoms and empires of the world are going to perish, for they are unable to take away even one measly little sin from the conscience of the afflicted and terrified sinner. The Jews should read their prophecies, and they will see that Christ came and ruled just as He promised.

At this time, the prophets had regard for holy Baptism and the preaching of Christ or the publication of the Gospel about Christ, when they foretold about the kingdom of Christ, Rom. 1: "...which He had promised by His prophets in Holy Scripture concerning His Son," as Daniel foretold most clearly ahead of the rest at this time of the authority or of the beginning of the kingdom of Christ, ch. 9 (as he says) unto the leadership [or authority] of Christ. He does not say "until the birth of Christ" but "until the Leader," that is, beginning through the Gospel, ruling out first His own mouth and then even "from the mouth of infants and nurslings," as we read in Psa. 8. The words of Daniel are: "Seventy weeks have been appointed upon your people and upon your holy city. Then your violation will be overturned, your sin will be covered, your iniquity will be atoned for. Eternal righteousness will be introduced, the vision and prophecy will be sealed, and the Holy of Holies, that is, your King, will be anointed." Know and understand, then, from the end of the discourse, that they will rebuild Jerusalem until the coming of Christ, the Leader, etc. To see a computation of these weeks, see the note of Luther on Daniel, as well as Philip [Melanchthon] in his *chronica carionis*.

Peter, too, repeats the same things in Acts 10 regarding this time and the beginning of the kingdom of Christ or the new testament and speaks a sermon to the Gentiles in the house of Cornelius, "which God sent to the children of Israel announcing peace through Jesus Christ (that is, the Lord of all)." He said: "You yourselves know abut this word that the report thereof was published in all Judea. The news began first in Galilee after the Baptism which John was preaching, that God anointed Jesus of Nazareth, that is, made Him King and Chief Priest by the Holy Spirit and with power, who walked about doing good and healing all whom the devil was oppressing, because God was with Him, etc." These things were more majestic and greater than the Jews dreamed and the flesh could see.

However, Christ begins His kingdom from Baptism, which He Himself received. A little later, He will establish it for the whole world, not only for the Jews, not only for males (as He did in the case of circumcision), that with this glorious and divine revelation at the Jordan which happened in the presence of the people who were flowing forth to John, such as never happened to earlier fathers and prophets, He might declare what great grace of God and heavenly glory He Himself had brought to the new testament through the Gospel. This He did for those whom the Law and the judgment of God had been crushing, that is, to miserable and desperate sinners.

Because heaven opened there above Christ, there is no doubt but that this happened with a great light and that the Father of lights preached from that light over the Light of the world, that is, over His Son, without whom all these things are merely darkness (John 1). With this discourse, which certainly is the very Gospel from heaven as the pulpit of the whole world, the Father commends His Son and not to the Jews in the temple, but to the whole world and to us with these magnificent words: "This is My beloved Son, in whom I am well-pleased." He is not saying these words for His or His Son's benefit, as you also read about another word of the Father in John 12, but for our benefit, as if to say: "You people here see My beloved Son in your own flesh, that is, who is like you, given to you. I give Him to you; I commend Him to you. He belongs to you as much as you want, if you will have accepted Him in faith (John 1). In this beloved One, you are pleasing to Me (Eph. 1). In this He will be pleasing to Me, and I will be pleased with you. You will have been received in Christ, not in the Law nor in your good works nor in any creature whether heavenly or other. 'The wrath of God remains on Him who does not believe in the Son' (John 3), regardless of how much wisdom and righteousness make you stand out (1 Cor. 1 and 2). Moreover, he who believes in this beloved One, is himself beloved and has eternal life regardless of how much sin has oppressed him, for these, along with damnation which is due to sin, are driven out in this Son. 'In Him dwells all the fullness of the Godhead bodily, and in Him you are perfected' (Col. 2). You all receive from this fullness of Him who is filled with grace and truth.

There is no other saint, nor has there ever been one who has not received grace for grace from him (John 1). After all, the Law was given through Moses, but that very thing is nothing to Him (2 Cor. 4). Moreover, grace and truth come through Jesus Christ."

This is the sermon of the Father concerning the Son which He delivered from heaven to earth. By it, He has declared His kingdom to us and had pronounced or consecrated Him both the eternal Priest (that is, Mediator) and Propitiator. This is the calling of Christ that in our flesh He begins to reveal that He Himself is the one Physician to whom you must listen and not listen to the doctrines of people nor of demons. As the Father also adds on Mount Tabor, "Listen to Him!," that He himself may become the salvation and redemption of the world and our wisdom, righteousness, sanctification, and redemption (1 Cor. 1), just as we read in Heb. 5 about this calling from the psalm. He says: "No one usurps honor for himself, but God also calls him as He called Aaron." Thus, Christ did not glory Himself that He might become Chief Priest. He rather glorified Him who had said to Him: "You are My beloved Son. This day I have begotten You." Elsewhere he says: "You are a Priest forever according to the order of Melchizedek."

Also present at this Baptism and revealed there was the entire Trinity, to wit, the mystery which was unknown to all and which only believers know and confess. The Father appeared in the voice; the Spirit, in the dove, not in substance but in appearance, the same Spirit who appeared in fire on the day of Pentecost. Who will doubt here that the angels were also present, submitting themselves to their Lord and wondering with joy at this grace which had been offered to the world?

All these things happened also in our Baptism which God consecrated to us, instituted for us, and commanded us. You see, when we receive Baptism into Christ, the heaven which the Law had closed opens to us. The Father pronounces that we are His children through Christ into whom we receive Baptism. The Holy Spirit regenerates us into a living faith, a trust in prayer, and a new life besides. Present here, too, are the angels who always, as Christ says, "desire to see the face of the heavenly Father." As Peter says, they have respect for those things which are given through Christ. They are joyful in heaven over one sinner who repents, according to the word of Christ.

We are not saying empty things, and we are speaking not without the Word of God, that you not say: "These things were done for Christ and not for us," for also in our Baptism the entire Trinity was present in the revelation of the Word, which is an external revelation to those who are receiving Baptism. Here the Word concerns the presence of the Trinity, because we receive Baptism by the institution and command of Christ in the name of the Father and of the Son and of the Holy Spirit. We confess this Baptism when we say: "I Believe in God the Father, in God the Son, who suffered for us, and in God the Spirit," from which faith, and not from Papist and other observances, stems and rises the holy catholic Church, the communion of saints. Here we have remission of sins, not through someone else but through Christ Jesus alone, who suffered for us under Pontius Pilate. Here we have the resurrection of the flesh to eternal life. That is how far the efficacy of our Baptism extends. Would that the doctrines of demons among the Papists and others not lead people away into another direction!

Therefore, you have the very glorious beginning of the kingdom of Christ. However, let us imitate the example of Christ which you see in Luke that, after receiving Baptism, we pray to and invoke the Father; for, just as we arrive at that grace not by our own merit, so also we shall not persist in our own powers nor care correctly for the matters which belong to our calling, which faith we confess with our prayer, for the person who prays wants to be safe under another's protection.

Christ advises this and says: "Watch and pray that you not enter into temptation." You see, when you become a Christian and when God calls you to some duty, you experience strange temptations and a thousand tricks of Satan that you not become what you are, that you not do what God has commanded, that in your calling you bring no gain to others. This is what you see in our Head, Christ, for, immediately after His Baptism and before His preaching, He is caught up into the greatest temptations, etc. Read the rest of the certainly very great egregious matters in this passage of Matthew in the booklet which contains the sermons of Luther on Baptism and which were written by Philip [Melanchthon] and our people about Baptism.

"I need to be baptized, etc." With these words, John yields to Christ his office and all his duties. Although he is very saintly, he counts himself a sinner and has confessed from whom he is what he is. He therefore says: "You must baptize me, etc.," just as John the Baptist himself says in John 1: "All of us (not only others but also I) have received of the fullness of Christ, etc." Because John was merely Christ's forerunner, therefore he a little later gives way with his own preaching and Baptism, something which we read in the following chapter in this way: "When Jesus had heard that John had been handed over, etc." The rest of the heavenly lights, or Lucifer himself, are hidden to us, as we seek the sun, etc.

"For thus it befits us, etc." See the *scholion* of Luther.

138

# COMMENTARY ON MATTHEW 4.

" Then Jesus was led up, etc." From His Baptism, Christ was going to begin His preaching of the Gospel, as we had said earlier on the basis of prophetic Scripture. First, the Holy Spirit led Christ away into the wilderness to be tempted by the devil. The devil tempted Him not only after a fast of forty days and nights but also throughout the forty days, as Luke writes, with other temptations which he did not write down but which, nevertheless, were all aimed at His not believing that He was the Son of God or that God cared about Him; at His falling from the Word of God and His vocation, but all this under the guise of the Word of God; and finally at His abandoning of the faith and defecting to the greatest ungodliness with a contempt for God, but under the name of the adoration or worship of God, and this on the basis of the doctrines of demons. The devil is always in the habit of soliciting the saints in this way.

That you may see with what concern and cleverness Satan acts here to hinder the good news of the glory of God or that kingdom of heaven, you need steadfast faith, the Word, and prayer, as we have advised earlier. You also need these that at the same time you may also see here that which Heb. 4 says about the Christ, our Savior and Chief Priest: "We do not have a Chief Priest who cannot share sufferings in our infirmities; but received temptation in all matters just as we do, but without sin. Let us therefore approach the throne of grace confidently, etc." In the same way also, Christ in John 16 gathers everything together and attaches a conclusion to His long discourse. He says: "I have spoken these things to you that you may have peace in Me. In the world you will suffer oppression, but trust in Me. I have overcome the world." He commands us to trust because He has conquered and overcome His temptations for us. Read all of Sirach 2.

They [the Papists] read this Gospel during Lent because of that fast. However, Matthew is not speaking of the self-chosen fast which has been a quite laughable fast among us, a fast which no necessity nor temptation compels, which has no command of God, and is accompanied by false faith and the determination of others, etc. (Our people as well as we have spoken about this often elsewhere.) Therefore we do not think it worth our while to repeat these things here, for it is enough to say that among the faithful the doctrines of demons have been disgraced from the Word of God.

The discussion here, in fact, concerns a fast of necessity, because Jesus, led as He was into the wilderness, became hungry. There was no food, nor could He have any there, but in the judgment of reason He had to die of hunger. You see, the angels come and minister to Him because human assistance was far away. Also, the Holy Spirit had led Him to that—and not through traditions nor monkish rule.

In the meantime, Satan solicits Him—poor and abandoned as Christ was—that because of human affliction and as so honored, at peace and wealthy, He might fall from faith and confidence in God. Paul speaks about this fast in 2 Cor. 6: "...in much patience, in tribulations, in necessities, in distresses, in beatings, in imprisonments, in rebellions, in hardships, in vigils, in fasts, etc."

Christ calls this fast "wrestling," as He includes under the expression "necessary fast" all the poverty, losses, distresses, and physical afflictions of the faithful. When the Pharisees and the disciples of John asked Him why His disciples did not fast, He responded: "The children of the bridal chamber cannot mourn so long as the bridegroom is with them. The time will come, however, when the bridegroom will be taken from them; then they fast." They will mourn then when they have suffered persecutions for confessing the Gospel of Christ.

We therefore shall speak here about the three temptations which Christ overcame with the Word of God for us, as you see, that we may also overcome them in the same way. But now we shall speak as our father, Luther, preached in the courts of our princes and of the cities of Schmalkalden in 1537, and not about the temptations of individual Christians (about which read the *postilla*), but about the temptations of our very dear mother, our holy Church of Christ, to which Christ says in John: "If they have persecuted Me, they will also persecute you." Elsewhere, He consoles her and says: "What you have done (either good or evil) for one of the least of these who belong to Me, you have done it unto Me." He said to Saul: "Saul, Saul, why are you persecuting Me?" In Zec. 2, He says: "He who touches you touches the pupil of My eye."

Therefore Christ is still fasting (that is, suffering and mourning in His members), for Satan does not rest against Him in his members. We are certain that Matthew has described here the temptations of the Church from her beginning to the end of the world in these temptations of Christ.

First, from the beginning, in the time of the martyrs, the devil has troubled the Church but (that I may speak in this way) that is a human devil, through "fasting," that is, through physical necessities, distresses, afflictions, persecutions by both Jews and Gentiles. This devil never cites nor produces a Word of God in order to deceive, as you see; but you recognize his obvious violence and the harm he inflicts. However, the devil merely commands the Church to exert herself only for the present necessity and to defect from the faith that she may do well. He says: "Tell these stones to become bread," that you may say to God in prayer: "This is nothing." Here God gave Constantine the Great as a comfort to the Church crying out to heaven. He forbade persecution, but he was overcome in a war by his co-ruler Licinius, who was a very fierce persecutor of Christians, as you read in the histories of the Church.

After this physical temptation, there follows a spiritual one; for, when the devil sees that He has been unsuccessful in this way, he approaches as an angel (namely, an angelic devil), as if with the Word. As you see, He cites Scripture that he may deceive. This is not that black devil here whom we recognize readily in murderers, but the handsome devil as he appears in heretics and who appears transformed into an angel of light. Heretics indeed began to sprout earlier through the wretched Ebion, Marcion and others; here, however, Arius and others held the rule. At first they suffered repression, but under Emperor Constantius, the son of Constantine, they grew so strong that scarcely two bishops or pastors survived as such in the East.

Here the devil is thinking in this way: "Although many may defect because of persecution, nevertheless I am gaining nothing, for the Church keeps growing. Therefore, I shall enter by a different way." He says: "You Christians endure all things because of the Word. 'Behold the Word,' and 'Thus it is written' are fine. I am not the devil, as I was earlier. I am not leading you into a profane place but into the holy city and above the temple." However, let us be careful, for He is not leading into the temple, but, as a liar and impostor, he is omitting it, when he cites the psalm: "…in all your ways," that is, "in your calling," that misled as we are, we may learn as if from his word to think against the true Word and, as we read here, to tempt God. The ways not of humans but of doves and sparrows are to fly in the air from the temple to the ground, etc. Here God has given His Church the Emperors Theodosius, Arcadius, and Honorius, who kept defending her against the Arians and others.

However, as in the first temptation there remained many deniers who remained in their faithlessness, so also here the blasphemy against Christ endured in many Arians until Mohammed along with his sect embraced this heresy and terrible blasphemy and made out of Christ what seemed good to reason all the way until today. This is the terrible judgment of God.

Third and finally, when this worm was detected through the Word and the Arian blasphemy had been condemned, Satan attempts his final temptation in these last days. For several centuries now, he has been strengthening the Antichrist and the Antichristian kingdom and says: "I shall give you all these things if you fall down and worship me." He is obviously bold with his assumed authority. Here he has no Word of God nor concern for Scripture, as you see. He is dealing here only with lies: "All these things belong to me, and with this wonderful promise I shall give them to you, but under this condition: 'If you fall down and worship me.'"

This now is the dignity and peace of the Church of which the Papists boast. Here it is not an angelic nor human but clearly a divine devil who wants us to worship and extol him above God, that is, above the Word and worship of God, according to Daniel and Paul. He invokes the Blessed Virgin and the saints and makes them his intercessors. He denies that Christ alone is the Justifier, but makes Him a judge instead of the Mediator. He teaches us to trust human righteousness, rules, works, and indulgences and subverts the Gospel of the glory of the great God and the use of the Sacraments. Out of the forgiveness of sins, he creates a mockery so that a person has the remission of sins if he is buried in a Franciscan cap, etc. He also makes heartfelt contrition, oral confession, and the satisfaction of works to be the remission of sins. But where here are Christ and His blood? How great is the abomination of Masses? The Papists not only do all these things as very religious, contrary to the commandments of God and the Gospel of Christ, but also they teach them against the rationale of very holy faith.

How can the devil accomplish all these things? Through this promise of his, as we read in Luke: "I shall give you all this power and the glory of all the kingdoms of the earth, because they have been handed over to me, and I give those to whomever I wish. If then You fall down and worship before me, all these will be Yours." That is: "You will be the Lord of kings and of all the goods of the world by my power and authority. Only teach a lie as a hypocrite and abandon the faith. Let Your belly be your God, and mammon your confidence. May the greatest glory be Yours. Pass decrees, statutes, rules, and the worship of God contrary to the commandments of God, contrary to the Gospel, contrary to the faith. Cause this lie to become the Word of God and obedience of the Gospel. Imagine the Church to be this, namely, the condemnation of the Word and Church of God. Try to take the kingdom and priesthood away from Christ, that you may mislead and oppress Christians under this title, etc. In this way, you will truly worship me."

"This may not appear so and, although you imagine another kind of worship, I shall give you excellent wages, honors, riches, power over emperors and over every power, contrary to the opinion of righteousness and holiness so that the wisest and most powerful people will fear your very useful monk. May those whom you wish to uplift flourish, abound, be saints and be canonized, or let those whom you want to condemn perish in hell. Fortified as you are with these ramparts, you will worship the god Maosim (that is, of ramparts), according to Daniel, against all the ramparts which resist you. You will worship scrupulously in gold and silver and precious stones, because I am the god of these. These I shall give you if I shall have become your god. You have no need for the Word of God but only of these ramparts, unless you wish to abuse the Word of God in favor of Maosim." Ugh! How terrible! How low have we fallen?

Isn't this worshipping the devil and falling away from God when we consider the doctrines of demons, as Paul calls them, holy and glorify them? Isn't it devil-worship when we defend those doctrines with the pretense of Scripture, hypocrisy, force, and weapons, that is, with these two works of the devil, lying and murder, but corrupt, blaspheme, and deny the Word of God and allow its persecution? Isn't this dethroning God and substituting the devil for Him?

Here, after the Roman beast made Charlemagne and his successors subject to itself, the Church had no emperor nor will she have a defender. At this time, the emperors cannot hate the foe of the Church, the Antichrist, seated in the temple of God, as Paul foretold, lest you look for him elsewhere after you have become his devoted servants, have been sent away from grace to kiss his very blessed feet at which this beast has often rendered a very wicked grace, as it excommunicates them and divests them of their empire and life.

In this temptation, however, Christ Himself wants to rise up in His own time as the Ruler of His Church against the kingdom of the Antichrist, that is, against false doctrines and murders, just as He now has begun to slay him with the Spirit of His mouth through the Gospel. You see this prophecy in this account of the third temptation; for here Christ repels Satan by Himself and says: "Go away, Satan!," something He did not do in the prior temptations.

Our mother, the Church, has endured these terrible things, but on the basis of this Gospel, we hope for the end of those evils now. You see, what Christ said to the devil, namely: "Go away, Satan!" His bride, the Church, recognizing as she has the kingdom of the Antichrist, says this through the preaching of the Gospel. The sheep of Christ slay Satan, for they hear the voice of their Shepherd and follow Him. In this way, Satan's kingdom is totally destroyed very quickly by the light of His coming.

The same Gospel also says with Christ against false adoration and false servitude or false worship of God: "You shall worship the Lord, your God, and Him alone shall you serve," just as the psalm says about Christ: "All kings will worship Him, and all nations will serve Him." We worship God in spirit and in truth, when we trust Him according to the promises of the Gospel and believe that God is our Father through Christ alone. We serve Him when each person acts according to his own calling and has a concern over what God has commanded him, not that each may be justified but for the glory of God and the advantage of our neighbor. As a result of such preaching, the doctrine of the Antichrist and trust in our own hearts must vanish.

We therefore hope, now that the end is near, that the angels will come to us and we to the angels in the eternal kingdom who already now are ministering to us. But may the kingdom of darkness—along with all the ungodliness of Turk, Papist, and others—be cast into the lowest hell. Amen! Read the rest in the *postilla*.

"When Jesus had heard..." This is what we said earlier, that John was the forerunner of Christ according to his own word: "This is the One who is going to come after me." The morning-star precedes the day and the sun. When the sun rises, the morning-star nevertheless is still visible. So also John is still preaching when the Sun of Righteousness rises on the earth. You see, John the Baptist was not thrown into prison immediately after the temptation of Christ, something which Matthew also does not say, but John first points to Christ (John 1). Also, Christ performs some miracles in the presence of His disciples and the people of Jerusalem (John 2 and 3). All this did not happen after the incarceration of John.

What we read here (that is, that Jesus departed into Galilee) we believe was that departure about which John writes in ch. 4, because John, as the last Evangelist, wrote what the other Evangelists had omitted. They scarcely touched on the first year of Christ's preaching except in passing and hardly with any order so that you don't know when it happened. For instance, in this chapter [Mat. 4] we read about the calling of four of the disciples, something which I think happened before John was bound, if you compare this with John 1. Matthew says that this happened, but he doesn't say when it happened but what followed: "He went about all Galilee..." Who does not see that in the account this coheres with what had gone before: "But when Jesus had heard that John had been handed over, etc."? For after the office of John, the Sun of Righteousness rises here, and the day which John had foretold began to give to the whole world a more excellent day.

However, Christ begins from Galilee according to the prophecy of Isaiah. Against detractors, we say that Matthew is citing correctly the passage of Isaiah [9:1], even if he should omit some words, as that "at the first time was lightly afflicted and at the last was more grievously afflicted." After all, he wanted to say nothing else but what Isaiah had said, namely, that the light had risen for the people in darkness, according to that statement: "The poor have the Gospel preached to them." The good news of the glory of God comes to the despairing without our work or merit, and those lands first saw that great Light which formerly had been covered up under the external darkness of the Assyrians and now beneath the internal darkness of Pharisaic and Antichristian teaching.

With reference to the external darkness, read the account in 2 Kings 15 and 17; for the Hebrews call "darkness" into all good fortune by an allegory, as in the psalm: "The Light has risen for the righteous person, and happiness for those who are upright in heart." (Read the rest in the sermon of Luther on Isaiah 9.) All the named things here [Isa. 9:1] pertain to the verb: "He saw," as: "He saw the land of Zebulon and he saw Naphtali according to the way of the sea beyond the Jordan"; "He saw Galilee of the Gentiles"; and "The people who sat in darkness have seen a great light, etc."

"From that time, etc." He begins from the preaching of John that he may approve it, and He now proclaims more clearly and, in fact, displays that kingdom of heaven about which John had preached that "Christ is the Lamb of God who takes away the sins of the world," about which preaching we have spoken before. In

Mark, Christ says: "The time has been fulfilled, and the kingdom of God is at hand. Repent and believe." Obviously he felt that now was the time for publishing the Gospel and the kingdom of the Messiah to which the prophets had been looking and which was in the first weeks of Daniel. The Jews were dreaming of a far different kingdom of the Messiah, but there clearly was nothing to that.

"Moreover, as He walked, etc." First, He calls His disciples that He might instruct them in the Gospel, and He strengthens their faith with His miracles, as you see later in ch. 10, something which He here promises them in these words: "I shall make you fishers of men." So also, the prophets had their disciples, and these are called "the sons of the prophets." That is, they became teachers among their people.

These disciples were not monks but married at an appropriate time and fathered children, as we read in 2 Kings 4 that some woman of the wives of the sons of the prophets kept crying out to Elisha. We must read the same thing from Hebrews, etc., something which we said against the fanatic spirits who despised the external Word and teaching because of their spirituality. As many as believe have received instruction from God, from the Holy Spirit, but not without the Word. Otherwise many hear the Word, but they don't believe it. God has not taught those. Thus people in the Church receive instructions through the Word, and later they are received as pastors and teachers in the Church. See the rest of our comments on this passage in our *postilla*.

"And He went about, etc." When Matthew came to the history, that is, to the preaching and miracles of Christ, he at the same time, includes everything as the sum and theme of the preaching and miracles of Christ and deals with them briefly. First, he says that Christ preached the Gospel of the kingdom throughout all Galilee. About this kingdom, we said earlier: "The kingdom of heaven is at hand." It is not an earthly kingdom as the Jews imagined, made ready not with weapons but with preaching, as we read in Psa. 8: "Out of the mouths of nursing babies you have completed praise and strength."

Second, Christ confirmed this Gospel by curing all illnesses and weaknesses, as we read later in ch. 11: "Tell John what you have seen and heard: The blind see, etc."

Third, after the report of the Gospel and the blessings of Christ had spread, matters occurred poorly and many crowds followed Christ, according to the prophecy of the patriarch Jacob, Gen. 49: "…until Shiloh come, to whom the people will adhere." Moreover, people flee from God through the Law, as the Jews around Mount Sinai, etc., that you may see here also that word of Christ from Isaiah: The poor will have the Gospel preached to them.

## THE END OF MATTHEW 4.

# TO THE READER.

After reading the above pages, read the commentary of Luther on Mat. 5–7 and other notes and the *postilla* of the same man on Matthew, that you not need anything more beyond my commentaries. After all, there is no end to writing books. People are now writing many. Although the books are not bad, nevertheless they are unnecessary for the understanding of Scripture. People occupy themselves so much in reading such works that they themselves have no time to read Holy Scripture.

However, our readings ought to incline in that direction that they lead the reader into the depths of Scripture that readers later may be able to say to themselves what the Samaritans said to the woman, John 4: "We now believe, but not because of your words, for we ourselves have heard (from Holy Scripture and the Word of God) and know that this is truly the Christ the Savior of the world."

You see, in this brief commentary on Mat. 4, the four wonderful quotations he cited. You also see that I sent the reader back to those things which I treated in my commentary on Jer. 31. These now are in common hands and yet the studious reader requires those more in considering Mat. 4 than in Jer. 31. I have been more zealous and careful to add here those very points from my commentaries on Jeremiah.

Jeremiah speaks as follows: "The word on High, etc." He is explaining what he had said before: "I shall turn their grief into joy." First, he speaks about the two tribes: "Their grief-stricken outcry is heard outside Jerusalem because the Babylonian army is laying waste to all things in Bethlehem and in all the surrounding areas.

The poor dwellers therein are perishing and are being carried off as prisoners into Babylon. Nothing remains there except the wretched surface of an unending desert. There Rachel weeps for her children and is unwilling to listen to consolation about her children, that is, her citizens, because regarding the dead there is no hope for life; nor for those carried off, hope for return." In the meantime, Jerusalem and the remaining fortified cities are suffering miserable fear, although still bearing up under siege for so long a time, as we read at the end of Kings.

Because they used to see and hear either a little before or under the actual siege that the Babylonians were devastating wretchedly the unfortified towns (among which was Bethlehem) and villages, and were killing or leading off their people; these were the beginnings of the captivity of the two tribes until in the third year Jerusalem herself was captured after she had begun to come under siege. Although enemies cannot capture fortified cities, nevertheless they can lay miserable waste to adjacent towns which have no power to resist, as the Turks did against Vienna and now are doing in Hungary. "There is no other one to fight on our behalf except You, our God."

He says that those evil calamities had to come first, but: "Don't weep, Rachel, for your children will return after seventy years when the promises of God are fulfilled, and they will rejoice in the Lord." Read the same things in Micah 4, where he says the same things. Rachel was the beloved wife of Jacob. She died along the way when they went up to Ephrata, that is, Bethlehem, when she gave birth to Benjamin. She was buried there in a field. There Jacob erected to stone marker. That place has been called "the Tomb of Rachel" until this present day, as the account in Gen. 35 speaks.

Therefore, Jeremiah[13] here is calling Bethlehem and all its surrounding area "Rachel," as St. Matthew also understands. People

---

13    Translator's note: The header begins to read "Commentary on Jeremiah." The printer Klug indicates that this is an erratum.

say that Rachel is mourning and weeping when the people in Bethlehem and all its confines mourn and weep. Here he is also alluding to the account of the death of Rachel. She indeed died in great sorrow because she called her son *BenOmi*, that is, "Son of Grief." However, the midwife said: "Don't be afraid, because you will have this son." His father Jacob called him *"Benjamen,"* that is, "Son of My Right Hand." Here the prophet says to the suffering Rachel, that is, to that land and through it to all the people who were going to suffer: "Let the sound of weeping cease. There will be a reward for your work, and your children will return. He who is called 'the Son of Sorrow' will be 'the Son of the Right Hand.'"

From Benjamin came the tribe which provided the first king, Saul, and later, with the tribe of Judah, Benjamin remained in the kingdom of David against the ten tribes which defected from the descendants of David. At that time, the kingdom of David was called "the kingdom of Judah," from the royal tribe. Finally, that tribe gave us the greatest apostle, Paul. He was first the Son of Sorrow to his mother, that is, to the Church (1 Tim. 1); but God the Father made him "the Son of the Right Hand," according to the prophecy of Jacob. Benjamin remains "the ravening wolf."

Furthermore, it is also not strange that Rachel is said to weep when the tribe of Judah, in whose fields she lies buried, weeps and when the tribe of Benjamin, to whom she had given birth as she died, weeps. Here now in her descendants truly was *BenOmi*, that is, the Son of Grief. Why else would she have wept when a hundred years earlier the line of Joseph, the firstborn of the earth, was carried off from the land of Israel, which land was also often called "the land of Joseph," etc.? You see how many there were for whom that good Rachel wept, whom the Spirit here comforts. It appears to me, however, that the prophet properly has regard here for the land of her burial and for that Son of Sorrow whom she bore there. Matthew also interprets "Rachel" in this way.

If you are asking here why the prophet wanted to mention especially Bethlehem, I answer that, although Bethlehem on the surface was a despised town, nevertheless it had this glory and once gave that king who was beloved of God, David, whose kingdom the prophets foretold would be forever, that is, which was completed in Christ.

Next, according to the prophet Micah, Christ, whom people were awaiting, would be born of the Jews in Bethlehem. This is the greatest glory, isn't it, for this otherwise despised town to be preferred ahead of other cities and ahead of Jerusalem herself? Micah says: "Bethlehem, you are indeed small, but out of you will come the Ruler of Israel." Therefore Matthew follows not the words of the prophet, but his meaning: "Bethlehem, you are not the smallest, although you are quite small in appearance. Why are you not the least? Because from you will come forth the Ruler of Israel, whom the prophet has been foretelling just now." Therefore all the Jews were waiting for their Messiah, the glory of the whole world and salvation, from Bethlehem, just as the priests also responded to Herod later.

Now, however, this hope, along with all the promises of God, seems to have perished when Bethlehem was destroyed and her people partly slain and partly carried off. Where they now say that Bethlehem is where Christ should be born, the Jews, from whom Christ should be born, have departed and perished. Because of our sins, the promises of God have perished: that's the way unbelief feels when affliction comes. The prophet therefore comforts and says that the promises of God cannot perish, for the Jews will return to Bethlehem and rebuild the town where Christ will be born according to the promise of God, and Israel will receive eternal consolation and glory.

What shall we say about the quotation of Matthew who cites this passage regarding Herod slaying the children in Bethlehem and in all its limits? Our response is an easy one if a person be unwilling to calumniate. Matthew says: "Then what the prophet Jeremiah had said has been completed, when he said: 'A voice in Rama, that is, on high, was heard, etc.'" Matthew is not denying that this had already happened before, just as we said, but he then is saying that which Jeremiah said happened when the children of Bethlehem were slain. Here again that happened which Jeremiah once foretold. Here again, Rachel weeps for her children in Bethlehem and in all its environs. A terrible outcry and weeping of fathers and mothers rose in Bethlehem and in her fields round about because of the slain children.

Why wouldn't Matthew cite the same passage when he again saw that that had happened which once happened according to the prophecy of Abraham? This is as if we shouldn't cite the psalms regarding our wretchedness, temptations, and salvation, which often have a different account.

The town of Bethlehem indeed was due this punishment in her children because the children there were living wickedly. Inhumanely, they kept denying a place in the inn for the girl Mary as she bore Christ in the night and in the midst of giving birth, as Luke writes of the Gentile magi who were announcing the birth, as Matthew writes, who had come to worship Him. The residents of Bethlehem did not seek him out to whom Herod directed that loss of their children and witnessed that the Messiah was born there, because of which he slew those infants.

However, comfort again comes to the afflicted: "Let the voice now stop weeping. Your children have been slain for Christ. That is good for them, and they will return in the final resurrection. Furthermore, Rachel, your children—that is, the residents who were carried off from God not by a change of place but by unbelief—will return from the kingdom of Satan when Christ and the apostles preach the Gospel, etc.," as we have said about a spiritual leading back. In this chapter, at the same time we gather also a physical leading back, and that through Christ as an eternal blessing for the people which was revealed after the Babylonian Captivity.

This could have been a very certain consolation: "Don't weep, for Christ has been born, and because of Him, Herod has slain the children. Therefore Christ is not just the Life-Giver for your children but also of all people according to the prophecies of the prophets."

In fact, later they were converted through the Gospel and even rejoiced over the slain children, congratulating them for this glory because it happened to them that they died for the sake of Christ even before confessing Him. They also began to say about Christ: "He is the One whom Herod feared, and for this reason he killed our children, one for you, two for me, and more for those having two mothers," and later: "O fortunate children, and fortunate us, who happen to have lived now, etc." For them, this was a comfort after their preceding affliction and terrible mourning.

However, because this second chapter of Matthew is filled with wondrous citations, and from it the godless Porphyrius and others charged the apostle falsely with ignorance; let us take this opportunity to speak about these quotations.

It could appear that in this chapter others who wanted to add some prophecy to all the accounts of Christ's childhood have added some things. However, it is not enough to say this because the Church of Christ, as we know, has always held the Gospel of Matthew as perfect and never dared change anything in it. The godly also have asked what they might say in a godly and appropriate way on these passages, which did not at all stop the calumnies of the wicked.

First, Matthew says that the priests and scribes cited: "And you, Bethlehem, in the land of Judah, etc." This passage from Micah indeed necessarily looks to Christ, but the words appear to be out of harmony. The prophet says: "You are small." Matthew relates: "You are by no means the least, etc." But this is creating a problem where none exists, as we judged a little earlier regarding these words.

Second, Matthew cites the following words: "I have called My Son out of Egypt," which we read in Hosea 11. This was said about the people of Israel, which is called "the Firstborn," that is, the beloved Son of God," Exo. 4: "My Son, the Firstborn of Israel." How, then, does this also fit the Child Jesus when the Father called Him back from Egypt? I respond as before. Matthew is not denying that that happened before, but says that this has happened now. That Scripture could not have been fulfilled perfectly, had God summoned His son Israel from Egypt and had not called His Son Jesus from it, because the latter is the true and natural Son, but the former is His son only because of the latter Son, just as all believers are the children of God because of Christ. Christ is the Firstborn among many brothers. As we read in Genesis, the fathers were compelled by necessity to enter Egypt, but then were led back therefrom into the land of Canaan because God recalled them, because Christ in His physical presence had been sent not for the Egyptians but for the Jews to perfect there the mysteries of our salvation in His flesh.

Therefore, if God is said to have called His Son out of Egypt when He summoned His people Israel from there through Moses, all the more now is it true that through an angel He recalled out of Egypt into the land of Canaan His Son, Jesus, who is co-eternal with the Father and without whom no one is a child of God and without whom all things are nothing. Therefore you see that Matthew has cited this not badly, for he wrote the Gospel of Christ not for false accusers but for the Christians to whom he was speaking. The Son of God was called out of Egypt much more truly here than He once was called. In the meantime, however, he denies that that happened when he asserted this. Rather, he said that it had already been completed when another Son of God other than Israel was summoned out of Egypt. This was the only-begotten Son of God. He was truly the Israel about whom Isaiah said, ch. 49: "You are My Servant Israel, whom I have given as the light of the Gentiles to be My salvation to the end of the earth."

Third, Matthew cites: "A voice in Rama, etc." We have treated this sufficiently.

Fourth, he cites that passage: "He will be called a Nazarene." He says that the prophets said this. We are certain that Matthew was not looking at the word "*neser*" or "*netzer*," that is, "flower" or "branch," as we up to this point are in the habit of citing the passage of Isa. 11: "…a branch will grow out of his root, etc." You see, the various peoples did not call Christ the "Flower" according to the prophets whom Matthew is citing. Rather, he was looking at the word "*nazir*," that is, "separated," "consecrated" or "sanctified," namely, that is, to the Lord, something which we say in German as "*geweiet*," except through abuse we see in this word only caps and cockroaches, etc., and the consecrated chalices, etc. You see, because "Nazareth" is not found in the Hebrew Bible from which we would be permitted to make judgments about the letters and syllables; it is reasonable that Matthew is looking to this in agreement with those things which I shall say.

We know from the Law (Num. 6) that those who were called "Nazarites" at the time of their consecration were so-called until they had fulfilled their vow. But Samson was a Nazarite from the womb of his mother until he died, and this by the command of God sent to his mother through an angel, as you read in Judges 13. For this reason, his mother herself received a command to abstain from liquor, wine, and unclean things lest she contaminate the fetus in her womb, according to the law of the Nazarites, that is, of the separated or segregated, or of those sanctified to the Lord. Such was also John the Baptist, as the angel declared: "He will drink neither wine nor liquor," but he was not a "*nazir*" or Nazarite from the womb of his mother, but also from the womb of his mother he was filled with the Holy Spirit, etc. Christ declared about him: "Among those born of women, no one greater than John the Baptist has risen."

If, then, we here have respect not for the word (that is, for its letters or syllables) but only for what it means, that is, separation or consecration by which anything has been set apart and consecrated to the Lord, as the Nazarites were consecrated to the Lord; then it is not at all strange that the prophets say about Christ that He was holy and consecrated to the Lord, although not a "*nazir*," but a "*cados*," that is, a holy person or a person whom another word will declare as holy, for He is the Son of God and true God, whom Isaiah (ch. 10) calls "the Holy One of Israel," or as David says: "I shall sing You a song on my harp, O Holy One of Israel." The law of primogeniture has respect for Christ: "Every male which throws open the womb will be called 'holy to the Lord,'" as Luke quotes from Exo. 34. See the law of primogeniture concerning those who are sanctified and separated for the Lord (Exo. 14).

But what need is there for me to say more? Daniel (ch. 9) calls Christ "the Holy of Holies, who is our sanctification"; in 1 Cor. 1, Paul calls Him "that Seed of Abraham in whom all the nations of the earth will receive blessing," who not only is the Firstborn among many brothers (Rom. 8), but also, whether you look at His divinity or humanity, holds the first place in all (Col. 1). Christ has this name of holiness in heaven and on earth, and to Him we also sing: "…for You alone are holy." Jeremiah (ch. 23) foretells: "And this is the name which they will call Him— 'Our Lord and Justifier.'" Also, the angel said to Mary: "The Holy One who will be born of you will be called 'the Son of God.'"

However, because Matthew makes "Nazarene" out of "Nazarite," as does John in the legend on the cross of Christ and says that He is going to be called a "Nazarene," it seems that he appropriately considered first the words of the angel in Judges 13, who said about Samson: "He will be a Nazarite of God from his infancy and from the womb of his mother. He will begin to deliver Israel from the hand of the Philistines." In this way, Samson was the figure of Christ, who was the holy Sanctifier and Deliverer of His people, for, as the angel says in Matthew: "He will save His people from their sins." Here He is the "Sun of Righteousness, and healing is in His wings" (Mal. 4). As Samson among the Hebrews has a name from the sun, so this "Samson," Christ, is a Nazarite of God and not of the Law, as we read in John that He is "the Passover Lamb." He says, from Exo. 13: "You will not break a bone of it." "For Christ, our Passover, has been sacrificed" (1 Cor. 5). In this way they are indicating that in Christ every holiness which Luke commanded was fulfilled, and that in this way He is our Righteousness and Sanctification, who sanctified or offered Himself to the Father in the fragrance of sweetness. Whatever the Law has commanded us to offer to God, as sacrifices, expiations, oblations, vows, Nazarites—all this is Christ, the sacrifice and offering for sins and for cleansing and healing for us.

The Law used to create Nazarites with its observances for some time, but God commanded Samson to be a Nazarite from the womb of his mother for all his time. Moreover, the Holy Spirit filled John the Baptist in his mother's womb. But these men were conceived in sin. Christ, on the other hand, was the Perfector of every Nazarite feature, conceived as He was by the Holy Spirit from the Virgin as the Son of God and Holy of Holies, the Nazarite of the Nazarites, the Lamb without blemish and separated from the flock (Exo. 12 and 1 Cor. 5); "who takes away the sin of the world" (John 1); "separated as He is from sinners and made higher than the heavens" (Heb. 7).

"But," you say, "if the Evangelist seems to have considered that passage of Judges 13, how does it fit that he says that this was said through the prophets?" I respond. Had he considered only that one passage, nevertheless it would not be unfitting to say that it was said by the prophets. You see, after the books of Moses, which the Hebrews call "the Law," there come the books of Joshua, Judges, Ruth, and Samuel, that is, the first two books of Kings and Malachi; that is, the latter two books of Kings which we call the "prophets" in the Bible, but they call the latter "prophets." However, if anything is said once in some one of these books, they say that it is written in the prophets.

Again you say: "Why, then, did Matthew change the words of that passage of Judges 13? For where we read: 'He will be a Nazarene of God,' Matthew says: 'He will be called a "Nazarene."'" I respond. First, the apostles don't tarry over words because they are rendering for us the sense of the words of Scripture. Next, it also appears that he did that for a great purpose, namely, to advise us of all the things we have said earlier from Scriptures or the prophets about the consecration and sanctification of Christ, not only that such a One was going to exist, but also that people are going to acknowledge and preach or confess Him.

After all, He is not merely going to exist, but people will also preach and confess Him as consecrated and sanctified for the Lord, and as set apart from sinners: "Him who Himself committed no sin, nor was any deceit discovered in His mouth." I say, they will call and confess Him, each in His own language, as consecrated to the Lord, just as the prophets had foretold that confession of Christ on earth among people. They say: "They will call Him the Lord our Justifier, and His name will be called 'Emanuel,'" after which the angel Gabriel said: "He will be great (namely, among people, for He is great from eternity) and will be called 'The Son of the Most High.' The Holy Spirit will come upon you, and the power of the Most High will overshadow you. Therefore, that holy thing which is born of you will be called 'the Son of God.'" This is just as Christ foretells, John 5: "All people will honor the Son just as they honor also the Father."

As we said before, when the discussion involves the subject and not the words, you see how broadly that quote opens up: "He will be called a 'Nazarene'"; for he is considering that in the Law and the Prophets not only is all sanctification completed in Christ but also that people will call or preach Him as such, so that you see that Matthew did not say in vain that this was said by the prophets when he wanted to remind people of almost all the Scripture which concerns Christ. You see, His sanctification would have profited me not at all that He is the Lamb of God, who was separated from sinners and was a Nazarite truly and without the Law, even if He were not so called; that is, even if I were not to hear this through preaching, I would believe and confess and preach Him along with the faithful.

I have been saying these things about the subject of this word *"nazir"* as to what each faithful person in the world expresses about Christ to his own salvation and to the glory of the Father. Among His Hebrews, however, Christ was going to be called in the Hebrew tongue a "Nazarite," as Matthew wants this from Scripture, something which he could not and should not do according to the Law, for the sanctification and righteousness of Christ is not of the Nazarites nor of the Law. After all, no one sees Him observing the law of the Nazarites, lest we create for ourselves out of the life of Christ monastic rules against Christ and His Gospel or against the righteousness of faith. He drank wine, of which the Pharisees also accused Him for not being holy as was commonly foretold. If He were a Nazarite, He would not drink wine, so that you see from this what a great appearance of holiness the observed Law of God which concerned Nazarites had at that time.

Christ allowed this appearance of sanctity to others, and He gave to the very saintly John this appearance beyond human measure before people. He had not given signs and miracles to John as an approved man of a very holy and admirable life, who bore witness about Christ. The people of the Law believed him and wondered at such a kind of man so that at the same time they had no excuse for not believing him whom they kept judging as very holy and even suspected of being the Messiah, as we read in John 1: "He came to bear witness of the Light." But Christ did not need such an appearance, for He could show who He was with wondrous miracles, etc.

However, because the Hebrews or Jews were unable to call Christ a "*nazir*," that is, sanctified or consecrated, according to the law of the Nazarites, which He was not keeping; although He nevertheless was One for whom all sanctification of the Law had respect, which Law could not sanctify before God, because this glory was due to Christ alone; I say, because of all that, He was called after His home town with the name of His clan "*Nozri*," that is, a Nazarite or Nazarene, which clearly mean the same thing, that is, "sanctified" or "consecrated," because they are written with the same letters *zain*, and ought not be written with a *samech*. Thus He was given that name among people (although for a different reason), so that He was called what He truly was before God and which the world later was going to confess about Him, as we have said sufficiently earlier.

Because of this name, the scribes and Pharisees wanted to make Him suspect as if He were not the Christ because, as they had said, He had come from Nazareth and not Bethlehem (John 7 and 8). But Christ kept acknowledging that name freely, and the people kept calling Him "the prophet from Nazareth," which they interpreted as "separation" and "sanctification." Pilate attached to the cross of the Savior this name in Greek, Hebrew, and Latin letters. This was undoubtedly by the will and counsel of God. The apostles were not ashamed of that name because, after they had received the Holy Spirit, they preached His Gospel among the Jews. Peter spoke this way, Acts 2: "Jesus of Nazareth, a man, etc."; and in Acts 3: "In the name of Jesus Christ of Nazareth, whom you crucified, whom God raised from the dead, and who Himself stood up before you as sound."

They also preached Jesus of Nazareth among the Gentiles (Acts 10). In Acts 22, Paul tells that Christ had said that He had already been glorified: "I am that Jesus of Nazareth whom you are persecuting." In Acts 26, he says: "I used to think I would do many things by fighting against the name of Jesus of Nazareth, etc." For that reason, even now Christians are called "Nazarites" or "Nazarenes," but in a contemptible way as if those were fools who believed that He was the Messiah who had come from Nazareth and not from Bethlehem, as was said. In the same way, today we are called "Lutherans," so also then they were called "Christians." But we, too, now freely bear such names, and for that reason we go forth rejoicing. That's how far we are from bearing such names with a wicked spirit, until the truth should illumine even those who blaspheme such names, as that truth came to Paul or as judgment deservedly comes to many others.

You have the following about contempt for Nazarenes, Acts 24: "We have found this pestilential fellow Paul, who is preaching rebellion to all the Jews in all the world, and an instigator of the sect of Nazarenes." Paul himself seems to have acknowledged this name freely when he said in Rom. 1: "...separated for the Gospel of Christ"; and in Gal. 1: "...who set me apart from the womb of my mother," etc.

I have said all these things, and yet I have not delayed over those who wrote on the legend on the cross "Nozri" with a *samech*, for here there is a strange inconsistency in the writers for some write "Nozri" with a *zain*, as it ought to be written, and which was still written with a *zain* in the notes of Erasmus on the Gospel of Luke which were printed in Basel in 1520. They thought that those who were writing this title in the Hebrew considered it unimportant whether they wrote *"Nozri"* with a *samech* or a *zain*, provided that the word remain the same. This, however, they did poorly in my judgment, as if this prophecy ought to mean something to us. They care only about the word and think that what this word represents is unimportant.

Pagninus contends that in the translation of the New Testament we should write everywhere "Nazareth" and Nazarite" or "Nazarene" with an "s" and not a "z."[14] Why? Because it reads that way in Rome on the title of the cross where *"Nosri"* is written with a *samech*. Therefore they believe that the whole cross, even the title, was brought over from Jerusalem, as if Rome at that time truly did not overflow with such errors and lies. But the Evangelists all write it with a "z," something which confirms everything which we have said. (Read the *scholion* of Luther on Lev. 21.)

That we may finally close, let us listen also to Christ Himself about his "Nazarenity." He says, John 10: "If he called them 'gods' to whom the Word of God came, and if we cannot break Scripture, do you say that He whom the Father sanctified and sent into the world is a blasphemer because I said: 'I am the Son of God'?, etc." He says that the Father sanctified Him and sent Him into the world. You do not hear "a Nazarene of the Law of God" more truly than that Samson was one, and that the Father sent a Nazarene into the world to deliver His people, etc. Here you see again that Matthew did not tarry with the Lucianites and false accusers over this citation: "He will be called a 'Nazarite.'" Rather, he wanted to keep Christians at work.

For this reason, I was unwilling to satisfy the calumniators here, something which I saw I could not do. Rather, along with my Christian brothers on the occasion of this quotation, I wanted to enter into the broadest fields of Scripture to the glory of Christ, that, after I spoke in a godly way, I might also give others the op-

---

14    Translator's note: as Nasareth, etc.

portunity to examine more carefully the Scriptures which concern Christ. After all, we ought to know that the prophecies were given to believers and not to unbelievers.[15]

---

15    Translator's note: The printer Klug here adds two pages of errata, but I have corrected these as I translated.